For Machan,

DRIVE-BY SHOOTINGS
NEW YORK

David Bradford

Drive-By Shootings

David Bradford

text by Gerhard Waldherr

KÖNEMANN

© 2000 Könemann Verlagsgesellschaft mbH
Bonner Str. 126, D–50968 Köln

© Photographs: David Bradford

For the introduction by Verlyn Klinkenborg
© 1999 by the New York Times Co. Reprinted by permission.

Publishing and art direction: Peter Feierabend
Concept and design: David Bradford
Project management: Sally Bald
Assistant: Lucile Bas
Layout: Barry Wells
Fine art photographic printing: Kathy Kennedy
Translation into English: Michael Scuffil
Translation into French: Jean-Luc Lesouëf
Production: Mark Voges
Color separation: Typografik, Cologne
Printing and binding: Star Standard Industries Ltd.
Printed in Singapore

ISBN 3-8290-2891-1
10 9 8 7 6 5 4 3 2 1

CONTENTS

Dedicated to Gwen Welsh Bradford

and Lola

Yasothonsrikul

I would like to thank and acknowledge:

Barry Wells, Margaret Swendsied,
Don Westfield, Sally Henderson,
Yoash Tatari, Yasu Nakaoka, David Lida,
Mark Van Santen, Miss Helma,
Edgar Boevé, David Schilling,
Bradford Green, Guy Roberts
and the Tribeca Garage.

Thanks also go to:

Bernd Obermann, Michael Kunhenn,
Kris Dikeman.

...From time to time, as you cut across town on everyday business, New York's inherent theatricality seems to array itself before you with unusual economy, the grandness of the staging almost mocking the plainness of your business. You catch a morning cab to La Guardia, for instance, and instead of stiffing it out in midtown traffic, the driver bears north through Central Park on East Drive, edging upward along Madison Avenue, across 116th Street and finally onto the Triborough Bridge. In spring this is an inspired choice of routes, and the driver, gesturing at trees that will soon form a tunnel of green overhead, knows it.

...When the cab catches the Triborough on ramp, the city seems to revolve beneath you until it integrates these low rooftops with the taller buildings that lie beyond them. The river runs slowly downtown past the East Side's long flank. And all this theater lies threaded along the path of a single cab ride – the blaring chaos of midtown, the almost concupiscent pleasures of Central Park in spring, the vivid promptings and urgings of East Harlem. It seems forgivable, as you cross into Queens, to believe that it was arranged this way just for you. After all, tomorrow you will be an extra in someone else's epiphany.

...Manchmal ist man auf einer ganz alltäglichen Fahrt durch New York unterwegs, und plötzlich zeigt sich die Stadt mit größter Klarheit in all ihrer spektakulären Pracht, so daß einem das eigene Unternehmen vor so großartiger Kulisse geradezu lächerlich banal vorkommt. Man steigt zum Beispiel am Morgen in ein Taxi nach La Guardia, und statt sich in das dichte Gewühl des städtischen Verkehrs zu stürzen, nimmt der Fahrer den East Drive in Richtung Norden durch den Central Park, dann weiter die Madison Avenue, überquert die 116. Straße und erreicht schließlich die Triborough Bridge. Im Frühling ist das eine wunderbare Route, und der Chauffeur, der unterwegs auf die Bäume weist, die schon bald einen grünen Tunnel über der Straße bilden werden, kennt sich aus.

...Wenn das Taxi die Auffahrt zur Triborough Bridge erreicht, könnte man meinen, die Stadt drehe sich unter einem, bis die niedrigen Dächer der Vorstadt mit den höheren Gebäuden dahinter zur Einheit verschmelzen. Der Fluß strömt träge dem Zentrum zu, vorbei an der langen Flanke der Eastside. Und all das sind die Bilder einer einzigen Taxifahrt – das tosende Chaos der Innenstadt, die geradezu sinnlichen Freuden des Central Park im Frühling, das muntere Treiben von East Harlem. Wen wundert es, daß man drüben in Queens ankommt und das Gefühl hat, das Ganze sei nur für einen selbst inszeniert worden. Doch schon am nächsten Tag wird man Statist sein, wenn ein anderer das große Schauspiel genießt.

... De temps à autre, alors que vous traversez New York pour vaquer à vos affaires courantes, le caractère théâtral de la ville vous saute aux yeux si bien que la banalité de vos occupations paraît presque dérisoire face à la grandeur de la mise en scène. Un matin, vous prenez par exemple un taxi pour La Guardia, et plutôt que d'être immobilisé dans les embouteillages du centre ville, le chauffeur prend la direction nord, traverse Central Park sur l'East Drive, longe Madison Avenue, traverse la 116ᵉ Rue pour rejoindre la Triborough Bridge. Au printemps, cet itinéraire est merveilleux et le chauffeur le sait bien, qui désigne d'un grand geste les arbres qui bientôt se referment au-dessus de vous, tel un immense plafond vert.

... Lorsque le taxi s'engage sur le Triborough Bridge, on pourrait croire que l'on surplombe la ville jusqu'à ce que les toits des immeubles se confondent avec les bâtiments plus grands. Le fleuve paresse en direction du centre et s'étire le long d'East Side. Et sur le trajet d'une simple course en taxi tout un spectacle défile : la circulation anarchique et bruyante au centre ville, les plaisirs presque sensuels de Central Park au printemps, les appels et l'activité fébrile dans l'est d'Harlem. En arrivant à Queens, vous avez l'impression que toute cette mise en scène vous est destinée, à vous seulement. Quoi d'étonnant ? Dès le lendemain, vous n'êtes déjà plus que le figurant d'une revue à grand spectacle dont quelqu'un d'autre se délecte.

Verlyn Klinkenborg
New York Times
May 6, 1999

A Day

Photographer, Taxi Driver, or Both?
David Bradford on David Bradford

How would I introduce myself? That's not such an easy question. Okay, my name's David Bradford. I'm a taxi driver who takes photographs, and a photographer who drives a taxi. I'm two in one. I associate my photography with the taxi. My camera is always by my side when I drive. Outside the taxi, I take few photographs. After all, I spend six days a week on the job. Twelve hours a day. I never just think about picking up a fare, taking them somewhere and setting them down again. I always think about taking photographs too. For me it would be a waste to drive without my camera.

Recently I missed a splendid picture. I didn't take it, because I had run out of film. Damn! I messed up myself. I won't let it happen again. If I didn't take photographs, I would have to ask myself what I was doing in a taxi. It's not as if I were earning thousands of dollars a day this way. On the other hand, without the taxi I couldn't photograph the things I do photograph. Maybe I could earn my living as a professional photographer, but I like working from a vehicle. I like it when I don't know, when I'm taking photographs, what's going to happen the next minute. I feel like an esthetic detective.

I used to work as an art director in the advertising department at Saks Fifth Avenue. I worked on shoots which then appeared in national magazines and the *New York Times*. I had a good job, regular hours, two hours' lunch break (before I became an art director), holiday, social status. But sometime or other I just didn't want to be dependent on an employer anymore, to be on some payroll. Working for someone takes too much energy, takes away too much of the attention you give yourself. It's a distraction. It stops you pushing through to yourself. I found that frustrating. I asked myself what I could be doing if I spent 40 hours a week with David Bradford instead of Saks. There, I was helping to sell underwear or someone else's fashion. What for? What I wanted was to make closer contact with the things inside me and funnel this into my drawings.

At first I worked on the side as a bicycle messenger, but the money I earned from that was nothing to write home about. That's when I decided to drive a taxi. It was in February 1990. I decided to take pictures while driving around the city, which I could then use as a basis for my drawings. It had always been my goal in any case to make a career as a graphic artist. I didn't want to be a photographer, because it seemed to me to be too expensive with all the equipment one needs. I got my first camera from my sister. I thought, if I have an automatic camera with a good lens, I'd be able to take better pictures. I thought good pictures of the city would inspire me to draw even more quickly.

One day a fare on the back seat told me about a Yashica T4 with a Zeiss lens. 140 dollars. So I bought it. Maybe I had developed nine or ten rolls of film, when a guy from an advertising agency got in my taxi. He looked at my work, and said, "Wow, they're great. Come round, let's fix a date." He thought we should show the pictures to a daily news-paper. Three months after I had developed my first pictures, a man got into the taxi and asked if he could write an article for the *New York Times*. The piece appeared in 1993. A little while after, a director from German television phoned me. And a little while after that, CBS made a short film about me. I had exhibitions in a reputable New York gallery and in the Empire State Building. All I needed was a book. I always knew what it should be called: Drive-by Shootings. That's what I do: shoot the city from a taxi.

Sometimes I don't see much for days. Then again there are phases when I take photographs all the time. Do I think before shooting? I don't know, it's an automatic process, something that goes ahead by instinct. I think my subconscious tells me: "Photograph it!" I don't say, "Why?" I just photograph it. It's like shopping. I want this. I want that. I take it as a picture. I take photographs without looking through the viewfinder. I imagine what my hand sees. I imagine my hand to be my eye, and my car to be my moving lens. As a human being I'm limited in my movements, the car extends my radius of action, so to speak. Something that moves has a different reality from something fixed. I quickly discovered that my photos had a unique perspective, a certain balance which I sought in my drawings. For me it's like a composition by Mozart. One note fits the next.

The passenger compartment of my taxi always has two laminated pictures of mine hanging in it. And I always have my portfolio on hand, which I pass back if someone wants to see more. That happens quite often. From the outset, people reacted positively to my work. Then I knew I was on the right track. By now it's crazy how many people have already heard of me the first time they get in. They exclaim, "Wow, it's you!" But then who reckons on a cabbie who speaks English, is intelligent, and on top of it all, hangs interesting art in his cab? People don't expect an artist who drives a taxi to make art out of his taxi.

Once I had a trombonist from the New York Philharmonic. Another time the famous fashion photographer Richard Avedon was sitting on the back seat. He saw one of my pictures, praised it, and said I was an architectural photographer. It's amazing how people react when they realize I'm an artist. When people get in and say, "Oh, you speak English," I like to say, "Yes, but there is a surcharge." It's a joke of course. In the taxi business there aren't many American-born drivers left and nowhere in New York is there one who does what I do. I've invented something.

I think the success of my work is due to the fact that I'm simply in the right place at the right time and I know when to click. Added to that, I capture something in motion, while I myself am in motion. If I have a loaded camera, I feel powerful, plugged in and ready for any level of dialogue. Put another way, I'm not someone in the audience following a performance. I'm directing what's going to play a part in my pictures, and how. In order to be creative, you have to absorb the things you observe, let them work on you. It's a question of how you react to what's going on around you.

New York is the place for that. It's the crossroads, the intersections that everyone passes through, that make New York so exciting. There is always movement. You look at one thing and already something different is happening. You turn your head, and bang, again something new. There are still scenes which take my breath away and where I feel my heart pounding. It's like a dialogue with the city. She speaks to me. I speak to her. It's a pretty wild affair.

Fotograf, Taxifahrer oder beides?
David Bradford über David Bradford

Wie ich mich vorstellen würde? Das ist gar nicht so einfach. Okay, ich heiße David Bradford. Ich bin ein Taxifahrer, der fotografiert und ein Fotograf, der Taxi fährt. Ich bin zwei in einem. Ich assoziiere meine Fotografie mit dem Taxi. Meine Kamera ist immer bei mir, wenn ich fahre. Außerhalb des Taxis fotografiere ich selten. Schließlich bin ich sechs Tage im Dienst. Täglich zwölf Stunden. Ich denke niemals nur daran, Fahrgäste zu finden, zu transportieren und wieder abzusetzen. Ich denke immer auch ans Fotografieren. Für mich ist Fahren, ohne die Kamera dabeizuhaben, Verschwendung.

Neulich habe ich ein großartiges Bild verpaßt. Ich habe es nicht gemacht, weil ich keinen Film mehr in der Kamera hatte. Verdammt! Ich habe es selbst vermasselt. So etwas wird nicht wieder vorkommen. Wenn ich nicht fotografieren würde, müßte ich mich wirklich fragen, was ich in einem Taxi mache. Es ist ja auch nicht so, daß man täglich tausende von Dollar damit verdient. Andererseits: Ohne das Taxi könnte ich nicht das fotografieren, was ich fotografiere. Vielleicht könnte ich als Profifotograf meinen Lebensunterhalt verdienen, aber ich liebe es, aus einem Vehikel heraus zu arbeiten. Ich liebe es, wenn man beim Fotografieren nicht weiß, was im nächsten Moment geschieht. Ich empfinde mich als Detektiv in Sachen Ästhetik.

Früher war ich Art Director in der Werbeabteilung bei Saks auf der Fifth Avenue. Ich arbeitete an Aufnahmen, die dann in überregionalen Magazinen und der *New York*

Times erschienen. Ich hatte einen guten Job, geregelte Arbeitszeiten, zwei Stunden Mittagspause (bevor ich Art Director wurde), Urlaub, sozialen Status. Aber irgendwann wollte ich nicht mehr von einem Arbeitgeber abhängig sein, auf irgendeiner Gehaltsliste stehen. Für jemanden zu arbeiten, nimmt zuviel Energie, zuviel Aufmerksamkeit von einem selbst weg. Es lenkt ab. Es hindert einen daran, zu sich selbst vorzudringen. Das hat mich frustriert. Ich habe mich gefragt, was ich nicht alles tun könnte, wenn ich 40 Stunden pro Woche mit David Bradford verbringen würde statt mit Saks. Dort habe ich geholfen, Unterwäsche zu verkaufen oder die Mode anderer Leute. Wofür soll das gut sein? Ich wollte engeren Kontakt aufnehmen, mit dem, was in mir steckt und das in meine Zeichnungen schleusen.

Anfangs habe ich nebenher als Fahrradkurier gearbeitet, aber ich konnte damit nicht besonders viel verdienen. Dann habe ich beschlossen, Taxi zu fahren. Das war im Februar 1990. Ich beschloß, während meiner Fahrten durch die Stadt Bilder zu machen, die ich als Vorlagen für meine Zeichnungen benutzen wollte. Es war ohnehin immer mein Ziel, als Zeichner Karriere zu machen. In die Fotografie wollte ich nicht einsteigen, weil sie mir zu teuer erschien mit all der Ausrüstung, die man benötigt. Die erste Kamera hatte ich von meiner Schwester. Ich dachte mir, wenn ich eine automatische Kamera mit einem guten Objektiv hätte, könnte ich bessere Aufnahmen machen. Ich dachte, gute Aufnahmen der Stadt würden mich sogar inspirieren, schneller zu zeichnen.

Eines Tages erzählte mir ein Kunde auf dem Rücksitz von einer Yashica T4 mit Zeiss-Objektiv. 140 Dollar. Die habe ich mir dann besorgt. Ich hatte vielleicht gerade neun oder zehn Filme entwickelt, als ein Typ von einer Werbeagentur in meinem Taxi saß. Der sah meine Arbeiten und sagte: „Wow, die sind großartig, komm' vorbei, laß' uns einen Termin machen." Er meinte, wir sollten die Bilder einer Tageszeitung präsentieren. Drei Monate, nachdem ich meine ersten Fotos entwickelt hatte, kam ein Mann ins Taxi, der mich fragte, ob er einen Artikel bei der *New York Times* unterbringen dürfe. Der Artikel erschien 1993. Wenig später hat mich ein Regisseur vom deutschen Fernsehen angerufen. Wiederum kurz darauf hat die CBS einen kleinen Film über mich gedreht. Ich hatte Ausstellungen in einer angesehenen New Yorker Galerie und im Empire State Building. Alles, was mir fehlte, war ein Buch. Ich wußte immer, wie es heißen sollte: Drive-by Shootings. Das ist es, was ich mache: Ich schieße die Stadt vom Taxi aus.

Manchmal sehe ich tagelang nicht viel. Dann gibt es wieder Phasen, in denen ich unentwegt fotografiere. Ob ich denke, bevor ich fotografiere? Ich weiß nicht, es ist ein automatischer Prozeß, etwas, das instinktiv vonstatten geht. Ich glaube, das Unterbewußtsein sagt mir: „fotografiere es!" Ich sage dann nicht: „Hey, warum?", sondern ich fotografiere es. Es ist wie Shopping. Ich will dies. Ich will das. Ich hole es mir als Bild. Ich fotografiere, ohne durch das Objektiv der Kamera zu blicken. Ich stelle mir vor, was meine Hand sieht. Ich stelle mir vor, meine Hand ist mein Auge, mein Auto ist mein bewegliches Objektiv. Als Mensch bin ich limitiert in meinen Bewegungen, das Auto erweitert sozusagen meinen Aktionsradius. Etwas, das sich bewegt, hat eine andere Realität als etwas, das fixiert ist. Ich habe schnell entdeckt, daß meine Fotos eine einmalige Perspektive haben, eine bestimmte Balance, die ich in meinen Zeichnungen gesucht habe. Für mich ist das wie eine Komposition von Mozart. Ein Ton paßt zum anderen.

Im Fahrgastraum meines Taxis hängen immer zwei laminierte Fotos von mir. Und ich habe immer mein Portfolio dabei, das ich nach hinten reiche, wenn jemand mehr sehen möchte. Das kommt häufig vor. Die Leute haben von Beginn an positiv auf meine Arbeit reagiert. Da wußte ich, ich bin auf dem richtigen Weg. Inzwischen ist es verrückt, wieviele Leute schon von mir gehört haben, wenn sie das erste Mal einsteigen. Die rufen dann: „Wow, Sie sind das!?" Aber wer rechnet auch mit einem Cabbie, der Englisch spricht, intelligent ist und noch dazu interessante Kunst aufhängt? Die Leute erwarten keinen Künstler, der Taxi fährt, um Kunst aus seinem Taxi heraus zu machen.

Einmal hatte ich einen Posaunisten von den New Yorker Philharmonikern. Ein andermal saß der berühmte Modefotograf Richard Avedon auf dem Rücksitz. Er hat eines meiner Bilder gesehen, es gelobt und gemeint, ich sei ein architektonischer Fotograf. Es ist erstaunlich, wie die Leute reagieren, wenn sie erkennen, daß ich Künstler bin. Wenn die Leute einsteigen und sagen: „Oh, Sie sprechen Englisch", sage ich gerne: „Ja, aber dafür müssen Sie extra bezahlen." Es ist natürlich Spaß. Im Taxigeschäft gibt es nicht mehr viele Cabbies, die in Amerika geboren sind, und in ganz New York gibt es keinen, der das macht, was ich mache. Ich habe etwas erfunden.

Ich glaube, der Erfolg meiner Arbeit liegt darin, daß ich einfach im passenden Moment am richtigen Ort bin und weiß, wann ich abdrücken muß. Außerdem halte ich etwas fest, das in Bewegung ist, während ich selbst auch in Bewegung bin. Wenn ich eine geladene Kamera habe, fühle ich mich mächtig und bereit für jede Ebene des Dialogs. Anders ausgedrückt, bin ich dann nicht jemand im Publikum, der einer Inszenierung folgt. Ich entscheide, was auf meinen Bildern eine Rolle spielt und wie. Man muß die Dinge aufsaugen, die man beobachtet, sie wirken lassen, um gestalterisch tätig sein zu können. Es geht darum, wie du auf das reagierst, was sich um dich herum abspielt.

New York ist dafür der Platz schlechthin. Hier begegnen sich auf engstem Raum unheimlich viele Menschen, deren Leben sich für einen kurzen Moment überschneiden, kreuzen. Da ist immer Bewegung. Du schaust auf eine Sache und schon passiert etwas anderes. Du drehst deinen Kopf, bäng, schon ist wieder was Neues. Es gibt Szenen, in denen mir immer noch die Luft wegbleibt vor Begeisterung und ich mein Herz schlagen fühle. Es ist wie ein Dialog mit der Stadt. Sie spricht zu mir. Ich spreche zu ihr. Es ist eine ziemlich wilde Liebesaffäre.

Photographe, chauffeur de taxi ou les deux à la fois ?
David Bradford au sujet de David Bradford

Comment me présenter ? Ce n'est pas aussi simple que cela. OK, je m'appelle David Bradford. Je suis un chauffeur de taxi qui fait des photos et un photographe qui conduit un taxi. Je suis les deux à la fois. J'associe la photographie au taxi. J'ai toujours mon appareil photo près de moi quand je conduis. Une fois sorti de mon taxi, je photographie rarement. Je suis tout de même de service six jours par semaine. À raison de 12 heures par jour. Trouver des passagers, les transporter et les déposer n'est jamais mon unique préoccupation. Je pense toujours à l'action de photographier. Pour moi, rouler sans avoir avec moi mon appareil photo serait du gaspillage.

Tout récemment, j'aurais pu faire une photo splendide. Hélas, il n'y avait plus de pellicule dans l'appareil. Zut ! Je ne peux m'en prendre qu'à moi-même. Mais cela ne se reproduira plus. Plus jamais. Si je ne faisais pas de photos, je me demanderais vraiment ce que je fais dans un taxi. En effet, ce n'est pas avec ça que l'on peut gagner des milliers de dollars par jour. D'un autre côté, sans taxi, je ne pourrais pas photographier ce que je photographie. Peut-être pourrais-je gagner ma vie comme photographe professionnel, mais j'adore travailler depuis un véhicule. J'aime, quand je fais de la photo, ne pas savoir ce qui va se passer l'instant d'après. Parfois, j'ai l'impression d'être un détective de l'esthétique.

Auparavant, j'étais directeur artistique du service de publicité chez Saks. Saks sur la Cinquième Avenue. Je travaillais sur des photos qui paraissaient dans des magazines et dans le *New York Times*. J'avais un bon boulot, des horaires de travail réguliers, deux heures de pause pour le déjeuner (avant que je devienne directeur artistique), des congés payés, un certain statut au sein de la société. Mais, un jour, je n'ai plus voulu être dépendant d'un employeur, ni avoir de fiche de paie. Travailler pour les autres vous prend trop de cette énergie et de cette attention dont vous avez besoin pour vous-même. Cela distrait. Cela vous empêche de pénétrer jusqu'au plus profond de vous-même. Cela m'a frustré. J'ai réfléchi à tout ce que je pourrais faire si je passais 40 heures par semaine avec David Bradford au lieu de les passer avec Saks. Chez eux, j'ai participé à la vente de sous-vêtements et de créations de designers. Ça ou autre chose ! Mais je voulais être à l'écoute de ce qu'il y a en moi et l'exprimer par mes dessins.

Au début, j'ai travaillé accessoirement comme coursier à vélo, mais cela ne rapporte pas grand-chose. J'ai alors décidé de devenir chauffeur de taxi. C'était en février 1990. J'ai décidé de faire, pendant mes trajets à travers la ville, des photos que j'utiliserais ensuite comme sources d'inspiration pour mes dessins. De toute façon, faire carrière comme dessinateur a toujours été mon objectif. Je ne voulais pas me lancer dans la photographie parce qu'elle me semblait trop chère avec tout le matériel dont on a besoin. Mon premier appareil photo, c'est ma sœur qui me l'a donné. Je me suis dis que, si j'avais un appareil photo automatique avec un bon objectif, je pourrais faire de meilleures photos. Je pensais que de bonnes photos de la ville m'inspireraient, que je pourrais dessiner plus vite.

Un jour, un client assis sur la banquette arrière m'a parlé d'un Yashica T4 avec objectif Zeiss. 140 dollars. Je m'en suis donc acheté un. J'avais peut-être développé tout juste neuf ou dix bobines de film lorsqu'un type d'une agence de publicité est monté dans mon taxi. Il a regardé mes photos et s'est exclamé : « Waoh, elles sont superbes, passe donc à l'agence, prenons rendez-vous. » Il pensait que nous devrions présenter les clichés à un quotidien. Trois mois après mes premières photos, un autre client a pris place dans le taxi et il m'a demandé s'il pouvait faire paraître un article dans le *New York Times*. Il a été publié en 1993. Un peu plus tard, un metteur en scène de la télévision allemande m'a appelé. Un peu plus tard encore, CBS a tourné un petit film à mon sujet. J'ai exposé dans une célèbre galerie de New York et à l'Empire State Building. Tout ce qui me manquait, c'était un livre. J'ai toujours su quel serait son titre : Drive-By Shootings. Et c'est ce que je fais : je prends des photos de la ville depuis mon taxi.

Parfois, je ne vois pas grand-chose pendant des jours. Puis il y a de nouveau des phases durant lesquelles je photographie tous azimuts. Est-ce que je pense à quelque chose avant de prendre une photo ? Je ne sais pas. C'est un processus automatique, quelque chose qui se passe instinctivement. Je pense que c'est mon subconscient qui me dit : « Prends ça en photo ! » Je ne pense pas « Hey, pourquoi ? », je photographie. C'est comme quand on fait du lèche-vitrines. Je veux ceci. Je veux cela. Je me le prends en photo. Je photographie sans regarder à travers l'objectif. Je m'imagine ce que voit ma main. Je m'imagine que ma main est mon œil, que mon auto est mon objectif mobile. En tant qu'homme, je suis limité dans mes mouvements, l'auto élargit en quelque sorte mon rayon d'action. Quelque chose qui a une autre réalité que ce qui est fixe. J'ai vite découvert que mes photos ont une perspective unique, un équilibre déterminé que l'on ne peut pas expliquer. Pour moi, c'est comme une composition de Mozart. Un son est en harmonie avec l'autre.

Dans le compartiment passagers de mon taxi, j'accroche toujours deux photos laminées que j'ai faites moi-même. Et j'ai toujours mon press-book avec moi, que je tends à ceux qui veulent en voir davantage. Cela arrive fréquemment. Dès le début, les gens ont réagi de façon positive à la vue de mes travaux. Je savais donc que j'étais dans la bonne voie. C'est incroyable de voir combien de gens ont déjà entendu parler de moi lorsqu'ils montent pour la première fois dans mon taxi. Ils s'exclament alors : « Waoh, c'est vous !? » Mais qui s'attend aussi à rencontrer un cabbie qui parle anglais, qui est intelligent et, en plus, expose des photos artistiques intéressantes. Les gens ne s'attendent pas à croiser un artiste qui joue les chauffeurs de taxi.

Un jour, j'ai transporté comme client un joueur de trombone de l'Orchestre philhar-monique de New York. Une autre fois, le célèbre photographe de mode Richard Avedon a vu quelques-unes de mes photos, en a fait les éloges et a déclaré que j'étais un photographe spécialiste de l'architecture. C'est étonnant de voir comment les gens réagissent quand ils s'aperçoivent que je suis un artiste. Quand ils montent à bord et disent : « Oh, vous parlez anglais ! », j'aime leur répondre : « Oui, mais il va vous falloir payer un supplément pour cela. » C'est une blague, bien sûr ! Dans la société pour laquelle je travaille, je suis le seul cabbie d'origine américaine. Naturellement, il n'y en a aucun, dans tout New York, qui fait ce que je fais. J'ai inventé quelque chose.

Je crois que le succès de mon travail réside dans le fait que je me trouve tout simplement au bon endroit, au bon moment et que je sais comment appuyer sur le déclencheur. De plus, je fixe pour l'éternité ce qui est en mouvement alors que je suis en mouvement. Quand j'ai un appareil photo chargé, je me sens fort et prêt à toute forme de dialogue. En d'autres termes, prêt à prendre une photo. Je ne suis pas quelqu'un dans le public qui obéit à une mise en scène. Je suis le metteur en scène. C'est moi qui décide ce qui joue un rôle sur mes photos, et comment. Il faut intérioriser les choses que l'on observe, les laisser agir avant d'agir soi-même en tant qu'artiste. Ce qui est important, c'est la façon dont on réagit à tout ce qui se déroule autour de soi.

À cet égard, New York est l'endroit idéal. Ici, une multitude d'êtres humains dont les vies se croisent pour un bref instant, se concentre dans un espace confiné. Il y a toujours du mouvement. Tu regardes quelque chose et, déjà, quelque chose d'autre se produit. Tu tournes la tête, bang, il se passe quelque chose de nouveau. Il y a encore et toujours des scènes qui me remplissent d'enthousiasme, me coupent le souffle et je sens mon cœur battre. C'est comme si je dialoguais avec la ville. Elle me parle. Je lui parle. C'est une passion tumultueuse.

BANANA REPUBLIC
YSTEMS
TIMES SQUARE
TIMES SQUARE
BROADWAY

A City like a Divine Spark
David Bradford on New York City

When I graduated from the Rhode Island School of Design in 1978, what I actually wanted was to go to Chicago. I used to live not too far from there, in Berwyn, Illinois. Just 20 minutes from The Loop. But then I thought, "If you want to go to a big city, you must go to New York." I came here with enough money for a week to start with, to find a job. At the end of the week I had a job, and I've stayed ever since. I'm glad I did. There are more opportunities here for anyone than anywhere else in the world.

I seek energy. And New York is energy, a festival of life, one big orchestra. New York is bustle and confusion. You can't take it in the way you can the countryside. It has skyscrapers and weather that passes through them as if they were mountains. Thunderstorms and snowstorms become almost surreal dramas. There are people here from every corner of the world, crisscrossing the place like pigeons. The buildings are just as colorful a mix as the people. There are big ones and small ones, beautiful ones and ugly ones. And there's the movement; syncopation. Cars, buses, trucks, sirens. There's never just one thing one has to cope with. The noise, the traffic, the stress, the people – they all flow into and out of each other. Everyone comes from everywhere, and they all bring some of themselves on to this tight little island.

The town is a river, and you are just part of a whole which is in motion. It is refreshing and heartening. I remember a particularly beautiful experience. It was a glorious day, the light was wonderful, and these majestic buildings all around me. And the radio was playing Beethoven's Ninth Symphony. "Freude schöner Götterfunken." Joy, beautiful divine spark. It was the perfect musical accompaniment to New York. When I think of New York I always have to think of music. Classical or Jazz. Jazz, with its syncopation, mimics NYC and classical music is a perfect accompaniment to dramas always unfolding here. Music is not just for the ears, but also for the pores. There's nothing better.

For a photographer, this is a wonderful playground. All I have to do is operate my camera correctly, the rest takes care of itself. Sure, the city has so much extraordinary architecture that a great deal of it has a certain balance and structure of its own. But between the buildings there move countless people, and out of this combination pictures arise like mystery plays. Let's just take my hand on the steering wheel. People ask, what's that? A spider perhaps? In some pictures, people or vehicles are transformed into reptiles in my eyes. Then again, some photos only reflect moods, they arise through different tones of light and shade, through glorifying sunshine.

I'm coming along from 8th Avenue, say. Downtown, going east. Ahead of me dawn lies over Manhattan. Grandiose. Or heavy rain, the middle of the night, a pair of lovers kissing in the dark. A magnificent feeling. Once a storm was raging, the rain was cascading over my windshield, blurring the lights and the outlines of buildings; people crouched behind umbrellas and looked as if they had lost out in the battle against the adversities of life and the city. A gigantic stage production. There are moments when I can hardly wait for someone to run in front of my lens. I play with everything that's out there. These shifted realities of the city, that's magical. When I photograph the snow in the park, you can hear the silence.

When I go to work in the morning, everything is still quiet. It's like a crescendo in music. By 7 o'clock, the tension is growing almost by the minute. More and more people arrive from New Jersey, they're spat out at the Port Authority bus station; the suburban trains from Long Island and the long-distance trains from Philadelphia and Washington D.C. arrive at Penn Station. People flood the sidewalks. Things can constantly happen which can change everything at a stroke. Events in this city can change destinies. One can feel everything in this city, even if one is not in direct contact with it. I haven't been to the opera or the theater for years, but I feel like I'm taking a part in a production each night and day. There's a lot going on.

I feel attracted to metal. One Sunday morning I was driving over the Manhattan Bridge and thought, "This could be a magnificent shot, all this iron – powerful, sober and yet sublime construction." I felt I was in the maw of the beast. I took two shots, one turned out great. New York's bridges are phenomenal. They are enormous sculptures. I love the Brooklyn Bridge. When the enchanting symmetrical tangle of the steel cables fly away from you above your head, you feel you no longer have your feet on the ground. But I like midtown too. The skyscrapers. The Citicorp Building, The Chrysler, Lever, Seagram and Grand Central Terminal. They are breathtaking temples of stone and glass. It's as though the people who built these buildings are speaking to us through them. "Look at what we've done."

New York buildings? They aren't modest buildings, plain residential complexes. No, they're statements. New York buildings are there to be seen. Like trophies. Like statues. Monuments designed to demonstrate pride and strength, a legacy of the time in which they were created. This city was built by men who wanted to leave a record of them-selves. Each generation has bequeathed something individual, something unique, and the process is continuing incessantly. New York is changing constantly at breakneck speed. I believe it's because everyone who lives here, whatever they do, wants to achieve something magnificent and special. And the result is this endless transformation to which New York is subject.

I have a few shots of Times Square, and the surrounding area known as Hell's Kitchen. They look like the image of an urban underworld. Mysterious, murky, dangerous. Seven or eight years ago, there was more filth, drugs, whores and gangs. Today it's a different world, changed beyond recognition. If people look at my pictures in a hundred years' time, they will be amazed. Just as we are amazed when we look at Paris as photographed by Adget. I have a volume of photographs of small towns in the USA at the beginning of the 20th century. You look at it and understand: that was their life, and it was quite different from our life today. I want to preserve the New York of today for posterity. If one does nothing with it, it is only in our heads, only a memory. We have to record it, in writing or some other form of expression. We have to freeze it, and thus keep it alive.

I love driving a taxi. I love driving down Broadway, Broadway is a great street. At any time of day. In any weather. South of Houston Street, I always think I'm plunging into the 19th century. Here I am in a 1998 "speeding" vehicle amongst buildings well over 100 years old and hearing music over 200 years old. Ah, New York City. Once I had this woman on the back seat, and she was really enthusiastic about my pictures. "Jeez, the more you look at them, the more you see. Who the devil is this Bradford?" I give people a feeling for this city, a feeling which they can connect with. I've received many compliments from my various passengers, but my fondest one was, "You make me feel proud to be a New Yorker."

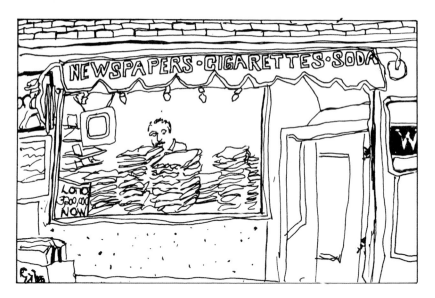

Eine Stadt wie ein Götterfunken
David Bradford über New York City

Als ich 1978 mein Studium an der Rhode Island School of Design abgeschlossen hatte, wollte ich eigentlich nach Chicago. Ich hatte vorher, nicht zu weit entfernt davon, in Berwyn, Illinois, gelebt. Nur 20 Minuten entfernt von The Loop. Aber dann dachte ich mir: „Wenn du schon in eine große Stadt willst, mußt du nach New York gehen." Ich kam dann mit genug Geld für eine Woche hierher, um einen Job zu finden. Am Ende der Woche hatte ich einen Job und bin geblieben bis heute. Ich bin froh, daß ich es gemacht habe. Hier gibt es für jeden mehr Möglichkeiten als an jedem anderen Platz der Welt.

Ich suche Energie. Und New York ist Energie, ein Fest des Lebens, ein großes Orchester. New York ist Hetze und Gewirr. Es ist nicht so überschaubar wie das flache Land. Die Hochhäuser wirken wie ein Gebirge. Aus Gewittern oder Schneestürmen werden beinahe surreale Dramen. Hier sind Menschen aus allen Ecken der Welt, die umherkreuzen wie Tauben. Die Gebäude sind so bunt durcheinander gemixt wie die Leute. Es gibt große und kleine, schöne und häßliche. Dazu kommt die Bewegung; dauernde Synkopen. Autos. Busse. Lastwagen. Sirenen. Es ist nie eine Sache alleine, mit der man fertig werden muß. Der Lärm, der Verkehr, der Streß, die Leute – alles fließt ineinander. Alles kommt von überall her, und alle bringen sich ein auf dieser kleinen, engen Insel. Die Stadt ist ein Strom, und du bist nur ein Teil des Ganzen, das sich bewegt. Es ist erfrischend und beglückend. Ich erinnere mich an ein besonders schönes Erlebnis. Es war ein herrlicher Tag, das Licht war wunderbar, um mich herum diese majestätischen Gebäude. Und im Radio spielten sie Beethovens Neunte. „Freude schöner Götterfunken". Es war die perfekte musikalische Begleitung für New York. Ich muß bei New York immer an Musik denken. Klassik oder Jazz. Jazz, mit seinen Synkopen, ahmt den Rhythmus der Stadt nach und klassische Musik ist eine perfekte Begleitung zu den Dramen, die sich in dieser Stadt immer wieder entfalten. Das ist Musik nicht nur für die Ohren, sondern auch für die Poren. Besser geht es nicht mehr.

Für einen Fotografen ist das hier eine wunderbare Spielwiese. Alles, was ich tun muß, ist meine Kamera korrekt bedienen, der Rest geschieht von alleine. Klar, die Stadt hat soviel außergewöhnliche Architektur, daß vieles von sich aus eine gewisse Balance und Struktur hat. Aber dazwischen bewegen sich unzählige Menschen, und aus dieser Verbindung entstehen Bilder wie Mysterienspiele. Nehmen wir nur meine Hand auf dem Lenkrad. Man fragt sich: Was ist das? Eine Spinne vielleicht? Auf manchen Fotos werden Menschen oder Fahrzeuge in meinen Augen zu Reptilien. Manche Fotos wiederum geben nur Stimmungen wieder, entstehen durch unterschiedliche Töne von Licht und Schatten, glorifizierendem Sonnenschein.

Ich komme zum Beispiel von der 8th Avenue, Downtown, fahre nach Osten, und vor mir liegt Manhattan in der Morgendämmerung. Grandios. Oder heftiger Regen, mitten in der Nacht, ein Liebespaar, das sich im Dunkeln küßt. Ein großartiges Feeling. Einmal wütete ein Blizzard, Regen lief in Kaskaden über meine Windschutzscheibe, davor zerflossen Lichter und Silhouetten von Häusern, Menschen duckten sich unter Regenschirmen und sahen verloren aus im Kampf mit den Widrigkeiten des Lebens und der Stadt. Eine gigantische Inszenierung. Es gibt Momente, in denen ich es kaum erwarten kann, bis mir jemand vor die Linse läuft. Ich spiele mit allem, was da draußen ist. Diese verschobenen Realitäten der Stadt, das ist magisch. Wenn ich den Schnee im Park fotografiere, kann man die Stille hören.

Wenn ich morgens zur Arbeit gehe, ist alles noch ruhig. Es ist fast wie ein Crescendo in der Musik. Bis 7 Uhr steigt beinahe minütlich die Spannung. Immer mehr Menschen kommen aus New Jersey, werden am Busbahnhof Port Authority ausgespuckt, aus Long Island kommen die Vorortzüge und aus Philadelphia und Washington D.C. die Fernzüge in der Penn Station an, Menschen überfluten die Gehsteige. Ständig können Dinge passieren, die schlagartig alles verändern. Ereignisse in dieser Stadt können Schicksale verändern. Man kann alles in dieser Stadt spüren, selbst wenn man nicht direkt damit in Kontakt steht. Ich war jahrelang nicht in der Oper oder in irgendeinem Konzert, und trotzdem habe ich das Gefühl, jede Nacht und jeden Tag an einer Produktion teilzuhaben. Es ist immer etwas los.

Ich fühle mich zu Metall hingezogen. Eines Sonntagsmorgens war ich auf der Manhattan Bridge unterwegs und dachte mir: „Das könnte ein großartiger Schuß sein, all dieses Eisen – eine kraftvolle, nüchterne und doch erhabene Konstruktion." Ich fühlte mich wie im Bauch des Wals. Ich habe zwei Fotos gemacht, eins davon ist brillant geworden. Die New Yorker Brücken sind phänomenal. Sie sind gewaltige Skulpturen. Ich liebe die Brooklyn Bridge. Wenn über einem dieses bezaubernde, symmetrische Gewirr der Stahlaufhängung dahinfliegt, fühlt man sich der Erde entrückt. Ich mag aber auch Midtown. Die Hochhäuser. Das Citicorp Building, das Chrysler, das Lever, das Seagram und der Grand Central Terminal. Es sind atemberaubende Tempel aus Stein und Glas. Es ist so, als ob die Leute, die diese Gebäude gebaut haben, durch sie zu uns sprechen. „Schaut her, was wir gemacht haben!"

New Yorker Häuser? Das sind keine bescheidenen Bauten, schlichte Wohnkomplexe. Nein, das sind Statements. New Yorker Gebäude sind da, um gesehen zu werden. Wie Trophäen. Wie Statuen. Monumente, die uns Stolz und Stärke demonstrieren sollen, ein Vermächtnis jener Zeit, in der sie entstanden sind. Diese Stadt wurde von Menschen gebaut, die Spuren hinterlassen wollten. Jede Generation hat irgend etwas Eigenständiges, Einmaliges hinterlassen, und es geht unaufhörlich weiter. New York ändert sich ständig, in einer rasenden Geschwindigkeit. Ich glaube, das liegt daran, daß jeder, der hier lebt, ganz egal, was er macht, etwas Großartiges, Besonderes erreichen will. Und dadurch entsteht dieser endlose Wandel, dem New York unterworfen ist.

Ich habe ein paar Aufnahmen vom Times Square, der Gegend drumherum, die Hell's Kitchen genannt wird. Die sehen aus wie die Inkarnation der urbanen Unterwelt. Geheimnisvoll, düster, gefährlich. Vor sieben, acht Jahren waren dort mehr Dreck, Drogen, Huren und Gangs. Heute ist das eine andere Welt, nicht mehr wiederzuerkennen. Wenn die Menschen in hundert Jahren meine Bilder sehen, werden sie staunen. Genauso wie wir staunen, wenn wir Paris sehen, wie es von Adget fotografiert wurde. Ich habe einen Bildband mit Aufnahmen von Kleinstädten in den USA Anfang des 20. Jahrhunderts. Man sieht das und begreift: Das war ihr Leben, und es war ganz anders als unser Leben heute. Ich will das New York von heute für die Nachwelt bewahren. Wenn man es nicht tut, bleibt es nur in unseren Köpfen, nur eine Erinnerung. Wir müssen es dokumentieren, indem wir es aufschreiben oder anderweitig ausdrücken. Wir müssen es einfrieren, nur so bleibt es am Leben.

Ich liebe es, Taxi zu fahren. Ich liebe es, den Broadway runterzufahren. Der Broadway ist eine großartige Straße. Zu jeder Uhrzeit. Bei jedem Wetter. Südlich der Houston Street denke ich stets, ich würde ins 19. Jahrhundert eintauchen. Hier bin ich nun in einem rasenden Wagen, Baujahr 1998, zwischen weit über 100 Jahre alten Gebäuden und höre Musik, die mehr als 200 Jahre alt ist. Das ist New York City. Einmal hatte ich diese Frau auf dem Rücksitz, und die war ganz begeistert von meinen Aufnahmen: „Jeez, je mehr man draufschaut, um so mehr sieht man. Wer zum Teufel ist dieser Bradford?" Ich gebe den Menschen ein Gefühl für diese Stadt, mit dem sie sich identifizieren können. Ich habe von meinen verschiedenen Fahrgästen viele Komplimente erhalten, aber mein liebstes ist: „Sie machen mich stolz, New Yorker zu sein."

Une ville comme une étincelle divine
David Bradford au sujet de New York City

Après avoir terminé mes études à la Rhode Island School of Design, en 1978, je voulais initialement aller à Chicago. J'avais auparavant vécu pas très loin de là, à Berwyn dans l'Illinois. Juste à 20 minutes du quartier « The Loop ». Puis je me suis dit : « Si tu veux aller dans une grande ville, c'est New York qu'il faut choisir. » Je suis donc venu ici, avec de quoi vivre une semaine, le temps de trouver un boulot. À la fin de la semaine, j'avais un boulot et je suis resté. Et je suis vraiment content de l'avoir fait. Ici, il y a, pour chacun, plus de possibilités que partout ailleurs.

Je recherche l'énergie. Et New York est énergie, c'est une hymne à la vie, un grand orchestre. New York, ses fébrilités et sa confusion. Avec ses gratte-ciel qui font l'effet de montagnes, on ne l'embrasse pas du regard, comme un pays plat. Les orages et les tempêtes sont le théâtre de drames presque surréalistes. Ici, les gens originaires des quatre coins du monde, vont et viennent comme des pigeons. Les bâtiments forment un kaléidoscope de couleurs, comme les êtres eux-mêmes. Il y en a des grands et des petits, des beaux et des laids. À cela s'ajoute le mouvement, la syncope. Des voitures. Des bus. Des camions. Des sirènes. Il faut toujours assimiler plus d'un élément à la fois. Le bruit, la circulation, le stress, les gens – tout s'entremêle. Tout arrive de partout à la fois et tous trouvent leur place sur cette petite île exiguë, à dimension humaine.

La ville est un courant, et tu n'es qu'un rouage dans le mouvement perpétuel. C'est rafraîchissant et gratifiant. Un souvenir particulièrement doux me vient à l'esprit. C'était une journée magnifique, la lumière était merveilleuse, et, tout autour de moi, ces bâtiments majestueux. Soudain, à la radio, ils se sont mis à jouer la Neuvième Symphonie de Beethoven. « L'Hymne à la joie ». C'était la transposition musicale parfaite pour New York. Quand je pense à New York, je pense toujours à la musique, au classique ou au jazz. Le jazz, ses syncopes nous restituent le rythme de New York City et la musique classique est un parfait accompagnement pour les drames qui s'y déroulent. Cette musique s'écoute et se vit tous les jours. C'est l'apothéose.

Pour un photographe, c'est ici un merveilleux terrain de jeu. Ma tâche consiste à utiliser correctement mon appareil photo, le reste va de soi. Bien sûr, la ville a une architecture si extraordinaire que l'ensemble des édifices crée un certain équilibre. Mais, une foule d'individus se déplace entre tous ces édifices et cette symbiose donne naissance à des tableaux qui ressemblent à des jeux mystérieux. Prenons seulement ma main sur le volant. On se demande : qu'est ce que c'est ? Une araignée peut-être ? Sur certaines photos, des hommes ou des véhicules apparaissent à mes yeux comme des reptiles. Certaines photos, en revanche, ne reflètent que des ambiances, qui sont le résultat de nuances de différentes densités de lumière et d'ombre, un rayon de soleil sublimant le tout.

Je reviens par exemple de la 8e Avenue, Downtown, je me rends vers l'est et sous mes yeux s'étend Manhattan dans le crépuscule du matin. Grandiose. Ou des averses violentes, en pleine nuit, un couple d'amoureux qui s'embrasse dans l'obscurité. Un feeling extraordinaire. Une fois, un blizzard faisait rage, la pluie tombait à flots sur mon pare-brise, et, devant moi, une mosaïque de lumières et de silhouettes, des passants courbés sous leurs parapluies et semblant mener une lutte sans espoir contre les adversités de la vie et de la ville. Une gigantesque mise en scène. Il y a des moments où j'ai du mal à attendre que quelqu'un croise mon objectif. Je joue avec tout ce qui se passe dehors. Ces réalités décalées de la ville, c'est magique. Quand je photographie la neige dans le parc, on peut entendre le silence.

Quand je me rends au travail, le matin, tout est encore calme. C'est presque comme de la musique qui va crescendo. Jusqu'à sept heures, on sent la tension monter presque d'une minute à l'autre. Du New Jersey débarque une foule de plus en plus compacte, déversée par la gare routière de Port Authority ; les trains de banlieue en provenance de Long Island et les trains longue distance de Philadelphie et de Washington D.C. s'arrêtent à la Penn Station ; une marée humaine envahit les trottoirs. Il se passe en permanence des choses qui transforment tout brutalement. Les événements qui se produisent dans cette ville peuvent modifier les destins. Tout est tangible en cette ville, même sans contact direct. Depuis des années, je n'ai mis les pieds à l'opéra, ni assisté à une pièce de théâtre et, malgré tout, j'ai la sensation de participer à une production jour et nuit. New york est pleine d'énergie et il est impossible d'y échapper.

Je me sens attiré par le métal. Un dimanche matin, je roulais sur le Manhattan Bridge et je me suis dit : « Ce pourrait être une prise de vue admirable, toute cette construction métallique froide, puissante, sobre, et, pourtant majestueuse. » Je me sentais comme dans le ventre de la bête. J'ai fait deux photos et l'une d'entre elles fut particulièrement réussie. Les ponts de New York sont fantastiques. Ce sont d'énormes sculptures. J'aime le Brooklyn Bridge. Lorsqu'au-dessus de vous est suspendu cet enchevêtrement magique et symétrique de câbles d'acier, vous avez l'impression que vos pieds quittent la terre. Mais j'aime bien aussi Midtown. Les gratte-ciel. Le Citicorp Building, Chrysler, Levo, Seagram et Grand Central Terminal. Ce sont des temples de pierre et de verre à vous couper le souffle. On a l'impression que les gens qui ont construit ces bâtiments vous parlent à travers eux. « Regardez ce que nous avons fait ! »

Les édifices de New York ? Ce ne sont pas de petits bâtiments modestes, des complexes locatifs à l'aspect banal. Non, ce sont des témoignages, ils véhiculent un message. Les bâtiments de New York sont là pour être vus. Comme des trophées. Comme des statues. Des monuments qui veulent nous faire une démonstration de fierté et de force, un héritage de l'époque à laquelle ils furent érigés. Cette ville a été construite par des hommes qui voulaient laisser des traces. Chaque génération a légué quelque chose de personnel, d'unique, et cela se perpétue indéfiniment. New York se métamorphose en permanence, à une vitesse incroyable. Je crois que cela est dû au fait que chaque habitant, quoi qu'il fasse, veut réaliser quelque chose de remarquable, de singulier. Et il en résulte cette mutation interminable à laquelle New York est assujettie.

J'ai pris quelques photos de Times Square, des environs, ce que l'on nomme la Hell's Kitchen, la cuisine de l'enfer. Cela évoque un univers interlope. Mystérieux, sombre, dangereux. Il y a sept ou huit ans, tout n'était que saletés et drogues, il n'y avait que putains et bandes de voyous. Aujourd'hui, c'est un monde différent, méconnaissable. Quand les gens verront mes photos dans cent ans, ils seront étonnés. Exactement comme nous le sommes en voyant Paris tel qu'Adget l'a photographié. J'ai un ouvrage photographique avec des prises de vue de petites villes américaines du début du XXe siècle. En voyant ces photos, on se dit : c'était leur vie et elle était totalement différente de la nôtre. Je veux préserver le New York d'aujourd'hui pour les générations futures. Si l'on ne fait rien dans ce sens, il n'en restera qu'un souvenir dans nos têtes, il faut l'enregistrer, le décrire ou l'exprimer d'une autre façon. Il faut le conserver afin qu'il reste en vie.

J'adore rouler en taxi. J'adore descendre Broadway. C'est une jolie avenue. Quelle que soit l'heure. Quel que soit le temps. Au sud de Houston Street, je m'imagine toujours que je plonge dans le XIXe siècle. Je suis au volant d'une voiture rapide, datant de 1998, au milieu de bâtiments vieux de cent ans et j'écoute une musique vieille de deux cents ans. Ah, New York ! Une fois, il y avait cette femme assise sur la banquette arrière et elle était littéralement emballée par mes prises de vue : « Ça alors, plus on les regarde, plus on découvre de détails. Qui diable est ce Bradford ? » Je suscite chez les gens un sentiment pour cette ville, un sentiment auquel ils peuvent s'associer. Je reçois de nombreux compliments de la part de mes différents clients, mais le plus cher à mes yeux est le suivant : « Grâce à vous, je suis fier d'être New-Yorkais. »

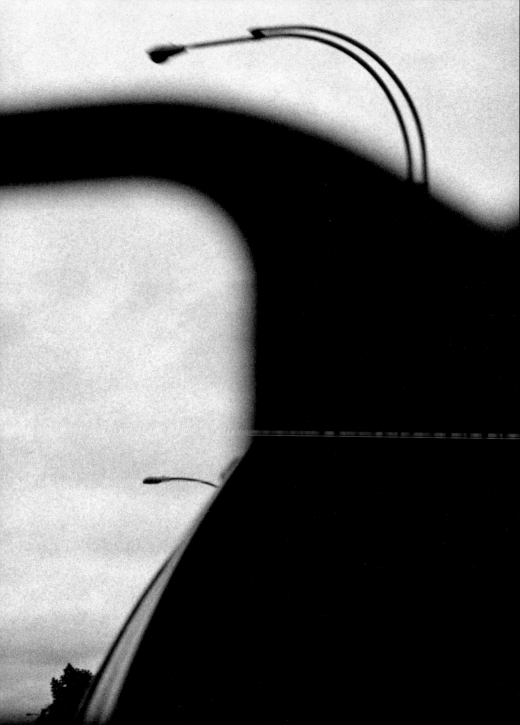

Drive, Look, Click and Flash
How Snapshots from a Taxi Became a Book

Now that Lola's not around anymore, his days have got a bit more lonesome. He gets up, has a cup of tea, eats a bowl of oatmeal, and an apple or a banana. Then he reads the newspaper or writes in his notebook. Maybe the generator for the air-conditioning is clattering in the backyard. Once you've gotten used to it, you don't hear it anymore. The fire truck sirens hardly bother him anymore either. The fire station's just a few blocks away but you get used to everything. David puts on a Buddy Holly record. He likes Buddy Holly a lot, and after all, the music disturbs no one. He has no family, no children, and his partners rarely stay long. Of course it's all down to this stupid job with its unsocial hours. But that can't be helped. He calls it slim living.

It's Saturday, 3.30 a.m. David Bradford, 47, is about to leave. First, 10 minutes' quick relaxation on the slant board set up in the kitchen. David says that it does the body as much good as an hour's sleep. Then he packs his briefcase with his street plan of the five boroughs and a water bottle filled with cleaning fluid for the windshield, pulls a baseball cap over his head, and puts on his glasses with the thick black frames. They make him look a bit like Buddy Holly himself. Outside it's chilly, the beginning of November. David says New York's particularly beautiful at the beginning of November. Somehow the city and the month go well together. He knows New York in all its nuances.

On the corner of 21st Street and 8th Avenue David meets two night owls and a down-

and-out with a shopping bag full of empty cans. He was mugged near here once on the way to work. Two men wrestled him and snatched his briefcase. David ran after them. He often runs. He has taken part in a number of 10K's and two marathons, one in New York, one in Philadelphia. Anyway, on that occasion he ran after the thieves, who dropped the briefcase. David says, "Whenever I pass this corner, I think of it. I think you never forget anything you've consciously experienced."

Outside the A&M deli there are a few Latinos standing around smoking. "Hi, David. Long time no see. What's Lola doing?" asks one. David goes into the shop, the assistant winks at him through the thick plexiglas screen and without being asked pushes a roll of Kodak Tri-Ex 400 through the opening above the counter. 3 dollars 70 cents. David puts the film in his briefcase, next to the Yashica automatic with its Zeiss lens. It's a ritual that David and the assistant have gotten used to. It's repeated six times a week, each time David passes by on his way to his garage in the west of Manhattan.

East West Management, Taxi Hire. This is the taxi company he works for. There's his usual vehicle, the Medallion with the license-plate number 6K23, in which he spends twelve hours each day. He pays a daily hire-charge of 120 dollars, and every day he puts the two black-and-white photos sealed in plastic in the back of the cab beneath his driver's license no. 444826. The calling cards of a man with a curious passion. As Bradford puts it, "I do drive-by shootings. I shoot the city from out of my taxi. That's what I do."

In the fall of 1993, the *New York Times* simply thought it'd be interesting "to see the city through the eyes of a cabbie." And that was doubtless not unrelated to the fact that New York cabdrivers are mysterious if not mystic figures, and their 12,000 yellow vehicles icons of the city. The reputation of the cabbies is legendary; they occupy a space between modern robber-barons and lunatics with driver's licenses. Bradford says, "Much of this is cliché, but certainly we're the focus in the nerve network of the city. At first this may have attracted additional attention to my work."

Meanwhile he has long since established a reputation as an artist, with two exhibitions in New York behind him. His photos have appeared in *New York Magazine, LIFE, Esquire* and in calendars. German television made a 45-minute film about him, and recently the fashion designer Donna Karan promoted Bradford on four pages in her first catalogue. In May 1998, the *New York Times* discussed Bradford's work on its arts pages and captioned a mysterious and soulful picture of Queensboro Bridge silhouetted against the sky with the words "Art is long, life is short".

Bradford's pictures unmistakably depict New York, but sometimes a New York which presumably no one has ever seen. The George Washington Bridge combined with the steering-wheel to form a magically symmetrical construct. The pinnacle of the Empire

State Building appears to have parted company with the rest of the building above a strip of cloud. Skyscrapers turn into toy boxes when reflected in car windows. A glance out through the cab windshield in Lincoln Tunnel looks as if one were being sucked into a postmodern underworld.

Bradford's photographic road movie is also poetic, however, and in total as strife-torn and contradictory as the city itself. Some of the shots record scenes and squares and reflect moods which one would not have thought the city capable of: sublime pitch-black gnarled branches against the backdrop of the East River during a thunderstorm, park benches apparently slumbering beneath snow, oriental magic with American neon signs in Chinatown. Tulips in the flowerbeds along the center of Park Avenue. Bradford has an eye for the contrariness of New York. One of these diametrical snapshots is a photo taken in Central Park. As cyclists pass a jogger, the moving car appears to stand still, while its windows reflect the jogger, cyclists and the trees as they stagger against each other.

A graduate of Rhode Island School of Design, David Bradford came to New York in 1978 intending to make a career as an illustrator and graphic artist. He got a job in the advertising department of the exclusive Saks Fifth Avenue department store, where he rose to become an art director. During his daily lunchtime walks, he photographed buildings and street scenes, which he used as the basis for his drawings. At some point or other he tired of the politics of his nine-to-five job and decided to try his hand as a freelance artist. Bradford said, "I knew when I did that I would have to make sacrifices, but I could not withdraw from the energy of this city."

The energy of New York consists not least in the urge of New Yorkers to continually change their lives, a compulsion to realize their greatest ambitions and goals. New York strives restlessly for better, more beautiful, richer, higher things. And Bradford is no exception. For the next year and a half he freelanced illustration and graphic design. And while he enjoyed greater freedom in the workplace, the money was not steady enough. So he started driving a taxi. "It left me with some independence." The independence to fulfill himself as an artist. The camera was his companion. When Bradford collected his first roll of developed film, he was pleasantly surprised. His astonishing discovery: "The photos were instant drawings."

It is 3.45 on this Saturday morning, when David Bradford leaves the garage. He says he can make 80 dollars by 6 o'clock if he's lucky. And he certainly can't afford not to be. 100 dollars clear profit after 12 hours in the car represents a good average for a New York cabbie, but for David Bradford, it is the bare minimum. The drive is hectic. Nothing but braking, moving off, braking, cornering. A rival tries to cut across. "You jerk!" Business is bad. In a resigned tone, Bradford says, "The taxi is my prison." And isn't he a bit like a prisoner? He takes a break at about 10 in the morning. Half an hour.

Until then, if he needs to, he takes a piss in a bottle he's brought along. The hunt for fares, the hunt for subjects – the daily routine, sometimes the daily torture.

The Manhattan meat packing district. Here there are in-places like Florent, very popular among night owls as the final stop. Here you can round off the night with a hamburger and a cup of coffee. There's not much going on outside Florent tonight. Bradford's cab bumps along past gay clubs and chic diners between brick warehouses. He says, "My eyes are constantly roving, they crisscross the city. At every red traffic light I try to fix on some object." The light changes to green, Bradford puts his foot down, a group of strong figures outside the Manhole Club, dim light, behind it a dark, oppressive gulch of houses. Bradford holds his camera out of the window at shoulder height. Releases the shutter. Flash. His first shot of the day. Quietly, the camera buzzes and winds the film on. Another of these inimitable pictures that show something that no one but him would have seen.

When he was six years old, David Bradford was hit by a car. He had serious head injuries, was in a coma for a long time, and regained consciousness with memory gaps and speech problems. "From then on, I lived more and more in my imagination, my fantasy." Skyscrapers seem to him like "ocean creatures made of stone." In high-rise buildings he sees "portraits of people; they reflect decades of people, the era in which they were built." In his pictures, the city is always bigger than its inhabitants, who come across as strangely lost. Two prostitutes in the side-mirror, framed by a deep black hole. An old Russian woman in rubber boots in the snow beside a garbage-truck. Passers-by who vainly seek to make headway against the driving rain beneath deformed umbrellas.

The thing with the accident left a permanent mark on him. When David Bradford talks about his life, it is divided into two parts. Pre-accident. Post-accident. "The last thing I can remember," he says, "was that I jumped off the milk truck with the intention of being the first one at the bus stop." A '57 Chevy just happened to be doing 40 mph in a 25 mph zone and David's head smashed the headlight of the Chevy, he himself was thrown fifteen feet and landed in the grass with his skull cracked, his brain exposed through a gaping wound. The milkman covered it with a handkerchief. The school bus came. The ambulance came. A piece of David Bradford was left behind. He says, "They all thought I was dead. In the hospital they put my chances of survival at fifty-fifty. I returned both the same and different."

David's father is a minister now and was at the time. And David says, "That's why lots of people prayed for me. Thousands of prayers. Even after I regained consciousness, they kept on praying for me. I believe prayers can heal and help. I believe the prayers saved me." The operation left a vertical scar beside his left eye, which had to be sewn inside and out with 500 stitches.

The rest was a slow feeling-back into reality. For little David, words and communication were no longer the most important thing. After all, language had partly abandoned him. There were many things he could no longer remember. They no longer had any significance in his social coordinate system. He sought new forms of expression. And that's how it stayed until long after David had grown up. He studied dance, did choreography, performed gymnastics, began to draw; drawing without looking at the paper. Blind contour drawing. The money paid out by the insurance after the accident, he invested in art school. Today he says, "Everything I have ever done in my life comes together in my present work: the feeling for spaces, the ability to use my hand as a tool, to do several things at once without losing sight of the context."

In April 1998 David came from his morning break and got into his taxi. At the next corner, a group of three got in, including Ralf Daab, the New York manager of the Könemann Publishing Company of Cologne, Germany. Daab saw Bradford's pictures. David gave him a copy of the article about himself in *LIFE* magazine, which he had long been using as a calling card. But in his experience, "Many never call back." This time was an exception. It was the birth of Drive-by Shootings. Ralf Daab says, "This kind of photography has never been seen before. The combination of taxi driver and photographer is unique."David Bradford had been taking photographs for seven years. He had spent seven years shooting, knowing his photographs some day might make a unique book. "The only other chance of saying goodbye to cab driving would've been to win the lottery." Now he had made it. The fulfillment of a life's dream and the hope of a new start. "Maybe it'll be a bestseller," he thinks, and smiles. Then he would have more time for himself once more, maybe even time for a relationship. Pity that Lola was no longer around to see it. What's become of her? "Canine heaven," says Bradford.

Lola was a black labrador mix with Irish setter. He finds it hard to get over her death two years ago. He got her when she was two months old. They spent 16 years together. Two days after German television had finished its documentary on David, Lola died. Old age. He still remembers, as though it were yesterday, the day he took her to the vet. She had a merciful death. David says, "It is as though she knew the film would happen and stayed long enough to be in it and then to say goodbye."

Sometimes David sits in a diner in the neighborhood. Then he notes philosophical thoughts about Lola in his diary, compares her beauty with that of New York and why he can't escape from either. Then he writes sentences such as: "Lola is beauty. Beauty is pure. Beauty is also love. When I drive through the most spectacular urban form of the universe, I see order and disorder, beauty and lack of beauty. In all this I move quickly, very quickly, with my finger on the shutter release, in order to catch, to capture this beauty, this order. For nothing exists which is not recorded. Except within oneself."

Fahren, Schauen, Klick und Flash
Wie aus Schnappschüssen aus dem Taxi ein Buch wurde

Jetzt, nachdem Lola nicht mehr da ist, sind seine Tage ein bißchen einsamer. Er steht auf, trinkt eine Tasse Tee, ißt eine Schale Haferflocken und dazu einen Apfel oder eine Banane. Dann liest er die Zeitung oder schreibt in sein Notizbuch. Kann sein, daß im Hinterhof wieder das Stromaggregat einer Air Condition knattert. Wenn man sich daran gewöhnt hat, hört man das nicht mehr. Auch die Sirenen der Feuerwehrautos stören ihn kaum noch. Die Wache liegt nur ein paar Häuser weiter – aber man gewöhnt sich an alles. David legt eine Platte von Buddy Holly auf. Er mag Buddy Holly sehr, und die Musik stört ja niemanden. Er hat keine Familie, keine Kinder, selten eine längere Beziehung. Natürlich liegt es an diesem bescheuerten Job mit seinen ungünstigen Arbeitszeiten. Aber daran kann er nichts ändern. Er nennt das ein asketisches Leben.

Es ist Samstag, 3.30 Uhr morgens. David Bradford, 47, wird sich gleich auf den Weg machen. Zuerst 10 Minuten auf dem schräg gestellten Brett in der Küche entspannen. David sagt, das verwöhne den Körper wie eine Stunde Schlaf. Dann packt er seinen Aktenkoffer mit dem Stadtplan der fünf Boroughs und einer Wasserflasche, gefüllt mit Essigreiniger für die Windschutzscheibe, stülpt sich eine Baseballmütze über und setzt die Brille mit dem dicken schwarzen Gestell auf. Mit der sieht er selber ein bißchen aus wie Buddy Holly. Draußen ist es frisch, Anfang November. David sagt, New York sei besonders schön Anfang November. Irgendwie paßten die Stadt und der Monat gut zusammen. Er kennt New York in all seinen Nuancen.

An der Ecke 21st Street, 8th Avenue begegnen David zwei Nachtschwärmer und ein Obdachloser mit einer Einkaufstüte voller leerer Getränkedosen. Hier in der Nähe wurde er einmal auf dem Weg zur Arbeit überfallen. Zwei Männer griffen ihn an und entrissen ihm seinen Aktenkoffer. David rannte hinter ihnen her. Er joggt oft. Er hat bei einigen 10-km-Rennen teilgenommen und zwei Marathonläufe bestritten, einen in New York, einen in Philadelphia. Jedenfalls verfolgte er die Diebe, die irgendwann den Koffer fallenließen. David sagt: „Jedesmal, wenn ich an dieser Ecke vorbeikomme, muß ich daran denken. Ich glaube, man vergißt nie, was man bewußt erlebt hat."

Vor dem A&M Deli stehen heute ein paar junge Latinos und rauchen Zigaretten. „Hi, David, lange nicht gesehen. Was macht eigentlich Lola?" fragt einer. David geht in den Laden, der Verkäufer zwinkert ihm durch das zentimeterdicke Plexiglas zu und schiebt ungefragt eine Rolle Kodak Tri-Ex 400 durch die Öffnung über der Theke. 3 Dollar 70 Cent. David legt den Film in den Koffer, neben die automatische Yashica mit Zeiss-Objektiv. Es ist ein Ritual, an das sich David und der Verkäufer gewöhnt haben. Es wiederholt sich sechsmal pro Woche, jedesmal, wenn David morgens zu seiner Garage im Westen Manhattans unterwegs ist. East West Management. Taxiverleih. Das ist die Taxigesellschaft, für die er arbeitet. Dort steht auch sein angestammtes Fahrzeug, das Taxi mit dem Kennzeichen 6K23, für das er für zwölf Stunden täglich 120 Dollar Leihgebühr bezahlt, und in dem David unter der Fahrerlizenz Nr. 444826 im Fond des Wagens stets die beiden in Folie eingeschweißten Schwarzweißbilder anbringt. Visitenkarten eines Mannes mit einer kuriosen Leidenschaft. Wie Bradford sich ausdrückt: „Ich mache Drive-by Shootings. Ich schieße die Stadt vom Taxi aus, das ist es, was ich tue."

Die *New York Times* fand es im Herbst 1993 interessant, die Stadt „mit den Augen eines Cabbie" zu sehen. Und das hatte sicher auch damit zu tun, daß New Yorker Cabdriver mystische bis mysteriöse Gestalten sind und ihre 12 000 gelben Fahrzeuge Ikonen der Stadt. Der Ruf von Cabbies ist legendär und bewegt sich zwischen Raubrittern der Moderne und Wahnsinnigen mit Fahrerlaubnis. Bradford sagt: „Vieles davon ist Klischee, aber wir sind auf jeden Fall der Mittelpunkt im Nervengeflecht der Stadt. Anfangs hat das vielleicht zusätzliche Aufmerksamkeit auf meine Arbeit gelenkt."

Inzwischen hat sich Bradford längst als Künstler etabliert, zwei Ausstellungen in New York hinter sich; seine Fotos sind im *New York Magazine*, in *LIFE* und in *Esquire* sowie als Kalender erschienen. Das deutsche Fernsehen drehte einen 45minütigen Film, der im WDR ausgestrahlt wurde, und kürzlich hat sogar die Modedesignerin Donna Karan Bradford für ein Shooting gebucht und brachte ihn auf vier Seiten in ihrem ersten Katalog unter. Im Mai 1998 besprach die New York Times Bradfords Œuvre im Feuilleton und betitelte ein geheimnisvolles und stimmungsvolles Bild der Queensboro Bridge, die sich vom Himmel abhebt, mit den Worten: „Die Kunst ist lang, das Leben ist kurz."

Bradfords Bilder zeigen unverkennbar New York, aber manchmal so, wie man es vermutlich nie gesehen hat: Die George Washington Bridge verbindet sich mit dem Lenkrad zu einem magischen symmetrischen Konstrukt; die Spitze des Empire State Buildings scheint durch Wolkenfetzen vom Rest des Gebäudes abgetrennt; Wolkenkratzer verkommen hinter verspiegelten Fenstern von Limousinen zu Spielzeugkästchen; ein Blick aus der Windschutzscheibe des Taxis im Lincoln Tunnel wirkt wie ein Sog in eine postmoderne Unterwelt.

Bradfords fotografisches Roadmovie ist aber auch poetisch und insgesamt so zerrissen und widersprüchlich wie New York selbst. Einige der Aufnahmen dokumentieren Szenen, Plätze, reflektieren Stimmungen, die man der Stadt nicht zutrauen würde: erhaben wirkende pechschwarze, knorrige Äste während eines Gewitters vor dem East River, unter Schnee schlummernde Parkbänke, fernöstlicher Zauber mit amerikanischen Schriftzügen aus Neonlicht in Chinatown. Tulpen in den Rabatten auf dem Mittelstreifen der Park Avenue. Bradford hat ein Auge für die Gegenläufigkeit New Yorks. Einer dieser diametralen Schnappschüsse ist ein Foto aus dem Central Park. Radfahrer passieren einen Jogger, das fahrende Auto scheint zu stehen, in dessen Seitenfenster spiegeln sich der Jogger, die Radfahrer und die gegeneinander taumelnden Bäume.

David Bradford, Absolvent der Rhode Island School of Design, kam 1978 nach New York, um als Illustrator und Zeichner Karriere zu machen. Er bekam einen Job in der Werbeabteilung des exklusiven Warenhauses Saks an der Fifth Avenue, wo er bis zum Art Director aufstieg. Bei seinen täglichen Streifzügen in der Mittagspause fotografierte er Gebäude und Straßenszenen, die er als Vorlage für seine Zeichnungen benutzte. Bis er irgendwann von seinem 40-Stunden-Job genug hatte und er sich doch lieber als freier Künstler behaupten wollte. Bradford sagt: „Ich wußte, wenn ich das mache, muß ich Opfer bringen, aber ich konnte mich der Energie dieser Stadt nicht entziehen."

Die Energie New Yorks besteht auch aus dem Drang der New Yorker, sich ständig verbessern zu wollen, immerzu größere Ambitionen und Ziele verwirklichen zu müssen. New York strebt rastlos nach besser, schöner, reicher, höher. So auch Bradford. Für die nächsten anderthalb Jahre entwarf er freiberuflich Illustrationen und Graphiken. Er genoß zwar die größere Freiheit bei der Arbeit, doch die Einnahmen waren nicht regelmäßig genug. Endstation Taxi: „Es beließ mir einige Unabhängigkeit." Die Unabhängigkeit, sich als Künstler zu verwirklichen. Die Kamera blieb sein Begleiter. Als Bradford die ersten entwickelten Rollen Film abholte, war er überrascht. Seine erstaunliche Entdeckung: „Die Fotos waren wie aus dem Augenblick geborene Zeichnungen."

Es ist 3.45 Uhr an diesem Samstag, als David Bradford die Garage verläßt. Er sagt, bis 6 Uhr könne er 80 Dollar machen, wenn er Glück habe. Und er kann es sich nicht leisten, keins zu haben. 100 Dollar Reingewinn nach zwölf Stunden im Auto sind für einen New Yorker Cabbie ein guter Schnitt, für Bradford Existenzminimum. Die Fahrt ist hektisch. Nichts als Bremsen, Anfahren, Bremsen, Abbiegen. Ein Konkurrent versucht, ihm den Weg abzuschneiden. „Du Idiot!" Das Geschäft läuft schlecht. Bradford sagt resignierend: „Das Taxi ist mein Gefängnis." Und ist er nicht auch irgendwie ein Gefangener? Er macht nur eine Pause, gegen zehn Uhr vormittags. 30 Minuten. Bis dahin pinkelt er in eine mitgebrachte Flasche. Jagd nach Kundschaft, Jagd nach Motiven, die tägliche, manchmal quälende Routine.

Im Bezirk der Großschlächtereien Manhattans. Hier gibt es In-Lokale wie das Florent, als letzte Anlaufstelle bei Nachtschwärmern sehr beliebt. Hier kann man die Nacht mit einem Hamburger und einer Tasse Kaffee ausklingen lassen. Vor dem Florent ist heute nicht viel los. Bradfords Wagen holpert vorbei an Schwulenclubs und schicken Diners zwischen Lagerhallen aus Backstein. Er sagt: „Meine Augen wandern ständig, sie kreuzen durch die Stadt. An jeder roten Ampel versuche ich, ein Objekt zu fixieren." Die Ampel zeigt grün, Bradford gibt Gas, eine Gruppe kräftiger Gestalten vor dem Manhole Club, schummriges Licht, dahinter eine dunkle beklemmende Häuserschlucht. Bradford hält die Kamera aus dem Fenster, Schulterhöhe. Knipst. Flash. Sein erster Schuß heute. Leise surrt der Apparat und spult den Film weiter. Wieder eines dieser einzigartigen Bilder, das etwas zeigt, was außer ihm keiner gesehen hätte.

Als Sechsjähriger wurde David Bradford von einem Auto angefahren, er hatte schwere Kopfverletzungen, lag längere Zeit im Koma und wachte mit Gedächtnislücken und Sprachproblemen auf. „Fortan lebte ich immer mehr in meiner Vorstellungskraft, meiner Phantasie." Wolkenkratzer muten ihm an „wie Ozeankreaturen aus Stein", in hohen Häusern sieht er „Porträts von Menschen und der Ära, in der sie gebaut wurden". Auf seinen Bildern ist die Stadt immer größer als ihre Bewohner, die in ihr seltsam verloren wirken: zwei Prostituierte im seitlichen Rückspiegel, umrahmt von einem tiefen, schwarzen Loch; eine alte Russin mit Gummistiefeln im Schnee neben einem Müllwagen; Passanten, die sich vergebens unter deformierten Schirmen dem peitschenden Regen entgegenstemmen.

Die Sache mit dem Unfall prägte ihn dauerhaft. Wenn David Bradford über sein Leben spricht, teilt es sich in zwei Teile. Vor dem Unfall. Nach dem Unfall. „Das letzte, woran ich mich erinnern kann", sagt er, „ist, daß ich damals aus dem Milchlaster gesprungen bin, um der erste an der Bushaltestelle zu sein." Ein 57er Chevrolet fuhr gerade mit 64 km/h in einer 40 km/h-Zone – Davids Kopf zerschlug den Scheinwerfer des Chevy, er selbst flog drei Meter durch die Luft, landete im Gras mit offenem Schädel, das Gehirn entblößt durch eine klaffende Wunde. Der Milchmann legte ein Taschentuch darüber. Der Schulbus kam. Die Ambulanz kam. Ein Stück von David Bradford blieb zurück. Er sagt: „Alle dachten, ich sei tot. Im Krankenhaus gab man mir eine Überlebenschance von 50 Prozent. Ich kehrte sowohl verändert als auch unverändert zurück."

Davids Vater war damals wie heute Pfarrer. Und David sagt: „Deshalb haben viele Menschen für mich gebetet. Tausende von Gebeten. Selbst als ich das Bewußtsein wiedererlangt hatte, wurde immer noch für mich gebetet. Ich glaube, Gebete können heilen und helfen. Ich glaube, die Gebete haben mich gerettet." Die Operation hinterließ eine senkrechte Narbe neben dem linken Auge, die innen und außen mit 500 Stichen genäht werden mußte.

Der Rest war ein langsames Zurücktasten in die Realität. Für den kleinen David spielten Worte, Kommunikation nicht mehr die Hauptrolle. Schließlich hatte ihn die Sprache teilweise verlassen, er konnte sich an vieles nicht mehr erinnern, es hatte keine Bedeutung mehr in seinem sozialen Koordinatensystem. Er suchte nach anderen Ausdrucksformen. Das blieb so, bis David längst erwachsen war. Er studierte Tanz, machte Choreographie, betrieb Gymnastik, fing an zu zeichnen – er zeichnete, ohne auf das Blatt zu schauen. „Blind Contour Drawing". Er steckte das Geld, das die Versicherung für den Unfall zahlte, in ein Kunststudium. Heute sagt er: „Alles, was ich jemals getan habe in meinem Leben, kommt in meiner jetzigen Arbeit zusammen: das Gefühl für Räume, meine Hand als Werkzeug einsetzen zu können, mehrere Dinge gleichzeitig machen zu können, ohne den Blick für den Kontext zu verlieren."

Im April 1998 kam David Bradford von seiner vormittäglichen Pause und bestieg sein Taxi. An der nächsten Ecke stieg eine dreiköpfige Gruppe zu, darunter der New Yorker Geschäftsführer des Kölner Könemann Verlags, Ralf Daab. Daab sah Bradfords Bilder. David gab ihm eine Kopie des Artikels über ihn in *LIFE*, den er seit längerem als Visitenkarte benutzt. „Viele", so seine Erfahrung, „rufen allerdings nie wieder an." Diesmal war es eine Ausnahme, die Geburtsstunde von Drive-by Shootings. Ralf Daab sagt: "Meines Wissens nach hat es diese Art von Fotografie noch nie gegeben. Die Kombination Taxifahrer und Fotograf erscheint mir einmalig."

David Bradford fotografiert seit sieben Jahren. Sieben Jahre hat er Fotos gemacht und gewußt, daß seine Bilder einmal ein einzigartiges Buch ergeben könnten: „Die andere Chance, mich vom Taxifahren verabschieden zu können, wäre ein Lottogewinn gewesen." Endlich war es soweit. Die Erfüllung eines Lebenstraums und die Hoffnung auf einen Neuanfang. „Vielleicht wird es ein Bestseller", sinniert Bradford und lächelt. Dann hätte er wieder mehr Zeit für sich, vielleicht sogar Zeit für eine Beziehung. Schade, daß Lola das nicht mehr miterleben kann. Was aus ihr geworden ist? „Hundehimmel", sagt Bradford.

Lola war eine schwarze Labradorhündin gemischt mit einem irischen Setter. Es fällt ihm schwer, ihren Tod, der nun zwei Jahre her ist, zu überwinden. Er bekam sie, als sie zwei Monate alt war. 16 Jahre verbrachten sie gemeinsam. Zwei Tage, nachdem das deutsche Fernsehen seine Dokumentation über David abgeschlossen hatte, starb Lola.

Altersschwäche. Er erinnert sich noch wie heute an den Tag, als er sie zum Tierarzt brachte. Sie bekam einen gnädigen Tod. David sagt: „Es ist, als hätte sie gespürt, daß dieser Film gemacht würde und blieb lang genug, um in ihm mitzuwirken und dann ‚Goodbye‘ zu sagen."

Manchmal sitzt David in einem Diner in seiner Nachbarschaft. Da notiert er dann in seinem Tagebuch philosophische Gedanken über Lola, vergleicht ihre und New Yorks Schönheit und warum er von beiden nicht loskommt. Dann schreibt er Sätze wie: „Lola ist Schönheit. Schönheit ist pur. Schönheit ist auch Liebe. Wenn ich durch die spektakulärste urbane Form des Universums fahre, sehe ich Ordnung und Unordnung, Schönheit und den Mangel an Schönheit. Ich bewege mich in all dem schnell, sehr schnell, den Finger am Auslöser, um die Schönheit, die Ordnung einzufangen, festzuhalten. Denn alles, was nicht aufgenommen wird, existiert nicht. Außer in einem selbst."

Rouler, regarder, click et flash
Comment, à partir d'instantanés pris depuis un taxi, est né un livre

Maintenant que Lola n'est plus là, ses journées sont devenues un peu plus solitaires. Il se lève, boit du thé, mange un bol de flocons d'avoine, accompagnés d'une pomme ou d'une banane. Puis il feuillette le journal ou écrit dans son calepin. Possible que, dans l'arrière-cour, pétarade de nouveau le groupe électrogène d'une climatisation. Une fois qu'on s'y est habitué, on n'y prête plus attention. De même, les sirènes des camions de pompiers – leur caserne est à quelques blocs d'immeubles de là – ne le gênent pratiquement plus. On s'habitue à tout. David met un disque de Buddy Holly. Il aime beaucoup Buddy Holly, et, d'ailleurs, la musique ne gêne personne. Il n'a pas de famille, pas d'enfants, pas de liaison durable. Cela est dû à ce boulot de dingue avec ses horaires de travail impossibles. Mais il ne peut rien y changer. Il n'y a pas grand-chose dans sa vie.

Samedi, trois heures et demie du matin. David Bradford, 47 ans, va bientôt se mettre en route. Tout d'abord, dix minutes de détente sur la planche inclinée en travers dans la cuisine. David dit que cela repose autant qu'une heure de sommeil. Puis il saisit son attaché-case avec la carte routière des cinq boroughs, prend une bouteille d'eau remplie de détergent au vinaigre pour le pare-brise, se coiffe d'une casquette de base-ball et chausse ses lunettes à épaisse monture noire. Avec ces verres, il ressemble un peu à Buddy Holly. Dehors, il fait frais, début novembre. David trouve que la ville de New York est particulièrement belle à cette époque de l'année. D'une certaine manière, la ville et ce mois-là vont bien ensemble, pense-t-il. Il connaît New York avec toutes ses nuances.

À l'angle de la 21ᵉ Rue et de la 8ᵉ Avenue, David rencontre deux noctambules et un sans-abri avec un cabas rempli de canettes vides. Non loin d'ici, il a déjà été agressé une fois, alors qu'il se rendait à son travail. Deux hommes l'ont malmené et lui ont arraché son attaché-case. David s'est élancé à leur poursuite. À cette époque, il faisait encore souvent du jogging, participant à deux 10 000 mètres, à deux marathons, un à New York, un autre à Philadelphie. Quoi qu'il en soit, ce jour-là, il poursuivit les voleurs qui finirent par laisser tomber la mallette. David déclare : « À chaque fois que je passe à ce coin de rue, je ne peux m'empêcher d'y repenser. Je crois qu'on n'oublie jamais ce que l'on a vécu consciemment. »

Devant A&M Deli, quelques jeunes Latinos font le pied de grue et fument des cigarettes. « Hi, David, ça fait un bail qu'on t'a pas vu. Que devient Lola ? » demande l'un d'eux. David entre dans le magasin, le vendeur lui fait signe à travers le plexiglas de plusieurs centimètres d'épaisseur et lui glisse, sans qu'on le lui ait demandé, une bobine de Kodak Tri-Ex 400 à travers l'ouverture au-dessus du comptoir. 3 dollars 70 cents. David met le film dans sa mallette à côté du Yashica automatique avec objectif Zeiss. C'est une sorte de rituel entre David et le vendeur. Il se répète six fois par semaine, quand David se rend, le matin, à son garage à l'ouest de Manhattan.

East West Management. Location de taxis. C'est la compagnie pour laquelle il travaille. C'est là que se trouve sa voiture habituelle, le taxi à la plaque minéralogique 6K23. Il passe 12 heures par jour dans son taxi et paie pour sa location 120 dollars la journée. David accroche, à l'arrière de la voiture, sous sa licence de conducteur au n° 444826, les deux photos en noir et blanc sous film plastique, les cartes de visite d'un homme à la passion étrange. Bradford : « Je fais du drive-by shootings. Je prends des photos de la ville depuis le taxi, voilà ce que je fais. »

À l'automne 1993, le *New York Times* avait tout simplement trouvé intéressant de voir la ville « avec les yeux d'un cabbie ». Cela était certainement aussi lié au fait que les cabdrivers de New York sont des personnages mythiques, voire mystérieux, et leurs 12 000 voitures jaunes, des icônes de la ville. Les cabbies dont la réputation est légendaire s'apparentent aux bandits de grand chemin de l'époque moderne ou à des fous du volant. « Bien des choses que l'on raconte à notre sujet sont des clichés, dit Bradford, mais nous sommes en tout cas au centre du système nerveux de la ville. Au début, c'est peut-être pour ça que l'on s'est intéressé à mon travail. »

Bradford s'est depuis longtemps fait un nom en tant qu'artiste, avec deux expositions à New York à son actif, des photos publiées dans *New York Magazine*, *LIFE*, *Esquire* ainsi que sous forme de calendrier. La télévision allemande a tourné sur lui un film de 45 minutes diffusé par la WDR, chaîne de télévision allemande, et, tout récemment, la styliste de mode Donna Karan a consacré à Bradford quatre pages de son nouveau catalogue.

Quant au New York Times, il a évoqué en mai 1998 l'œuvre de Bradford et publié une photo mystérieuse et triste avec la silhouette du Queensboro Bridge dans le brouillard, ainsi légendée : « L'art est long, la vie est courte. »

Les photos de Bradford représentent la ville de New York, telle qu'on ne l'a probablement jamais vue : le George Washington Bridge compose avec le volant du taxi une construction symétrique magique ; au-dessus d'un lambeau de brouillard, la pointe de l'Empire State Building semble s'être détachée du reste de l'édifice ; derrière les vitres miroirs des limousines, les gratte-ciel font penser à un jeu de construction, un coup d'œil à travers le pare-brise du taxi dans le Lincoln Tunnel et on a l'impression d'être aspiré dans un monde interlope post-moderne.

Mais ce roadmovie du photographe Bradford est tout autant poétique et, dans l'ensemble, tout autant déchiré, contradictoire que la ville de New York elle-même. Quelques-unes des prises de vues campent des scènes, des places, qui sont le reflet d'ambiances que l'on ne soupçonnerait pas ici : des branches d'arbres noueuses noires comme jais pendant un orage éclatant devant East River, les bancs d'un parc semblant somnoler sous la neige, ou encore la magie de l'Extrême-Orient avec des inscriptions lumineuses typiquement américaines à Chinatown. Des rangées de tulipes qui ornent la bande médiane de Park Avenue. Bradford a l'œil pour souligner les antagonismes de New York. L'un de ces instantanés, en opposition diamétrale, a été réalisé à Central Park. Des cyclistes dépassent un jogger, la voiture qui roule semble être à l'arrêt et ses vitres latérales reflètent le jogger, les cyclistes et les arbres inclinés les uns vers les autres.

David Bradford, ancien élève de la Rhode Island School of Design, est venu à New York en 1978 pour y faire carrière comme illustrateur et dessinateur. Il s'est vu confier un poste au service de publicité de Saks, grand magasin de luxe sur la Cinquième Avenue, avant d'être promu directeur artistique. Lors de ses flâneries quotidiennes pendant la pause de midi, il photographiait des bâtiments, des scènes de rue, qu'il utilisait comme source d'inspiration pour ses dessins. Jusqu'au jour où il en a eu assez de son boulot de 40 heures, lui qui voulait plutôt faire ses preuves en tant qu'artiste indépendant. «Je savais que, si je me lançais, je devrais faire des sacrifices, dit Bradford. Mais je ne pouvais pas me soustraire au dynamisme de cette ville.»

L'énergie de New York résulte notamment de la tendance des New-Yorkais à vouloir constamment réaliser de grandes ambitions et de grands objectifs. New York aspire sans relâche à plus de qualité, de beauté, de richesse. Tout comme Bradford. Il a travaillé pendant un an et demi comme illustrateur et dessinateur free-lance. Alors qu'il appréciait pleinement cette liberté dans son travail, l'argent qu'il gagnait n'était malheureusement pas suffisant. Voilà pourquoi il a commencé à conduire un taxi : « Cela m'a permis de conserver mon indépendance. » La liberté nécessaire à son épanouissement d'artiste. Seul l'appareil photo est resté son compagnon de route. Lorsque Bradford est allé chercher les premières bobines développées, il a été agréablement surpris. Son étonnante découverte : « Les photos étaient des dessins instantanés. »

Il est 3 heures 45 ce samedi-là, lorsque David Bradford quitte le garage. Il déclare pouvoir gagner 80 dollars jusqu'à six heures, s'il a de la chance. Il lui en faudra. Cent dollars de bénéfice net au bout de 12 heures de voiture sont une bonne moyenne pour un cabbie new-yorkais, le minimum existentiel pour Bradford. Sa conduite est nerveuse. Toujours freiner, démarrer, freiner, bifurquer. Un concurrent tente de lui couper la route. Pauvre type ! Les affaires vont mal. Bradford ajoute avec résignation : « Le taxi est ma prison. » Et n'est-il pas en quelque sorte un prisonnier ? Il fait une seule pause, vers dix heures du matin. Une demi-heure. Jusque-là, il urine dans une bouteille qu'il trimbale avec lui. À la chasse aux clients, à la chasse aux motifs, la routine quotidienne qui est parfois une torture.

Dans le quartier des abattoirs de Manhattan. On y trouve des cafés branchés comme le Florent, très populaire en tant qu'ultime lieu de rendez-vous des noctambules. On peut y finir la nuit par un hamburger et une tasse de café. Aujourd'hui, tout est plutôt calme devant le Florent. La voiture de Bradford longe en cahotant des clubs d'homosexuels et des restaurants chics entre des entrepôts de briques. « Je promène mon regard sur tout, mes yeux scrutent la ville, dit-il. À chaque feu rouge, j'essaie de fixer un objet. » Le feu passe au vert, Bradford accélère, un groupe de types baraqués devant le Club Manhole, pénombre ; derrière, un pâté de maisons plongé dans une obscurité oppressante. Bradford brandit son appareil photo par la fenêtre, à hauteur d'épaule. Déclenche. Flash. Sa première prise de vue pour aujourd'hui. Dans un léger bourdonnement, l'appareil fait avancer le film d'une photo. De nouveau l'une de ces photos étranges révélant ce que nul, à part lui, n'aurait vu.

À l'âge de six ans, David Bradford a été heurté par une Chevrolet ; il lui en est resté de graves lésions cérébrales. Il est sorti d'un coma prolongé souffrant de trous de mémoire et de troubles de l'élocution. « Dès lors, j'ai vécu de plus en plus dans mon imaginaire, dans mes fantasmes. » Les gratte-ciel sont pour lui des « créatures d'océans en pierre » ; dans les immeubles, il voit « des portraits d'êtres humains ; ces édifices reflètent l'époque à laquelle ils ont été construits ». Sur ses photos, la ville domine ses habitants qui semblent bizarrement perdus en elle : deux prostituées dans le rétroviseur latéral, encadrées par un profond trou noir ; une vieille femme russe chaussée de bottes en caoutchouc et marchant dans la neige à côté d'une benne à ordures ; des passants qui, sous des parapluies déformés, cherchent en vain à se protéger de la pluie battante.

L'accident l'a marqué à jamais. Lorsque David Bradford parle de sa propre vie, celle-ci se divise en deux. Avant l'accident. Après l'accident. « La dernière chose que je puisse me rappeler, dit-il, c'est que j'ai sauté du camion du laitier avec l'intention d'arriver le premier à l'arrêt de bus ». Une Chevy datant de 1957 était en train de rouler à une vitesse de 40 miles à l'heure dans une zone limitée à 25 miles. Sa tête s'est fracassée sur le phare de la Chevy ; lui-même a fait un vol plané de trois mètres, atterrissant dans l'herbe avec le crâne ouvert et le cerveau visible au milieu d'une plaie béante. Le laitier l'a recouvert d'un mouchoir. Le car de ramassage est arrivé, puis l'ambulance. Une part de David Bradford est restée sur place. Il dit : « Ils ont tous cru que j'étais mort. Mon cerveau était mis à nu. À l'hôpital, ils m'ont donné une chance sur deux de m'en sortir. Lorsque je suis rentré à la maison, j'étais le même et pourtant, j'étais différent. »

À cette époque, le père de David était pasteur. Et David ajoute : « Beaucoup de gens ont prié pour moi. Des milliers de prières. Même lorsque j'ai eu repris connaissance, ils ont continué de prier pour moi. Je crois que les prières peuvent guérir, aider. Je crois que ce sont les prières qui m'ont sauvé. » La plaie, suturée à l'aide de 500 points, lui a laissé, sous son œil gauche, une cicatrice verticale.

Le reste a été un lent tâtonnement pour revenir à la réalité. Pour le petit David, les mots, la communication n'avaient plus d'importance capitale. En effet, il souffrait de troubles du langage. Il y avait beaucoup de choses dont il ne pouvait plus se souvenir, cela n'avait plus de signification dans son système de repères sociaux. Il s'est mis en quête d'autres formes d'expression. Et cela a continué alors que David était depuis longtemps devenu adulte. Il a fait des études de danse, s'est consacré à la chorégraphie, a pratiqué la gymnastique, a commencé à dessiner, sans regarder sa feuille : « Blind conture drawing ». L'argent que la compagnie d'assurances lui a versé pour l'accident, il l'a investi dans des études artistiques. Aujourd'hui, il dit : « Tout ce que j'ai fait à cette époque de ma vie ressort dans mon travail aujourd'hui : la notion d'espace, la capacité d'utiliser mes mains comme un outil, de faire plusieurs choses simultanément sans perdre de vue le contexte. »

En avril 1998, David Bradford revient de sa pause en milieu de matinée et prend place dans son taxi. Au prochain coin de rue, un groupe de trois personnes dont le P.D.G. de la succursale new-yorkaise de la maison d'édition Könemann de Cologne, Ralf Daab, monte à bord de son taxi. Daab regarde les photos de Bradford. David lui donne une copie de l'article que lui avait consacré *LIFE* et qu'il utilise depuis longtemps comme carte de visite. Il sait par expérience que « beaucoup ne rappellent jamais. » Cette fois, ce fut une exception, l'instant pendant lequel est né Drive-By Shootings. « À ma connaissance, on n'a encore jamais vu ce genre de photographies, déclare Ralf Daab, la combinaison de chauffeur de taxi et de photographe est unique. »

David Bradford photographiait depuis sept ans. Sept ans qu'il espérait que ses photos donneraient un jour naissance à un livre : « L'autre chance de pouvoir abandonner la conduite du taxi serait de gagner le jackpot au loto. » Mais ce jour est finalement arrivé. Le rêve de toute une vie qui s'accomplit et l'espoir d'un nouveau départ. « Peut-être ce livre deviendra-t-il un best-seller », déclare, pensif, Bradford avant de sourire. Il aurait alors plus de temps pour lui, peut-être même du temps pour une nouvelle idylle, « alors, je pourrais envisager d'arrêter de conduire. » Dommage que Lola ne puisse plus en être témoin. Qu'est-elle devenue ? « Elle est au paradis des chiens », dit Bradford.

Lola était une chienne labrador croisée avec un setter irlandais. Il a eu bien du mal à surmonter sa mort il y a deux ans. On la lui avait donnée alors qu'elle avait deux mois. Ils ont vécu 16 ans ensemble. Deux jours après que la télévision allemande eut terminé le documentaire sur David, Lola est morte. De vieillesse. Il se rappelle le jour où il l'a emmenée chez le vétérinaire comme si c'était hier. On lui a donné le coup de grâce. David déclare : « Mais je sais qu'elle pressentait l'imminence du film et qu'elle s'est battue jusqu'au bout pour y faire une ultime apparition. »

Parfois, David prend part à un dîner dans un restaurant de son voisinage. Alors, il note dans son journal des pensées philosophiques au sujet de Lola, compare sa beauté et celle de New York et explique pourquoi il n'arrive pas à se détacher de toutes les deux. C'est ainsi qu'il écrit des phrases comme : « Lola est la beauté. La beauté est pure. La beauté, c'est aussi l'amour. Quand je roule à travers la forme urbaine la plus spectaculaire de l'univers, je vois l'ordre et le désordre, la beauté et l'absence de beauté. Je me déplace à travers tout cela, très souvent, très vite, le doigt sur le déclencheur, pour capter la beauté, l'ordre, les immortaliser. Car tout ce qui n'est pas photographié n'existe pas. Sauf pour soi-même. »

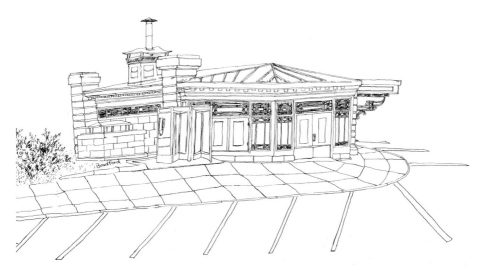

At Night

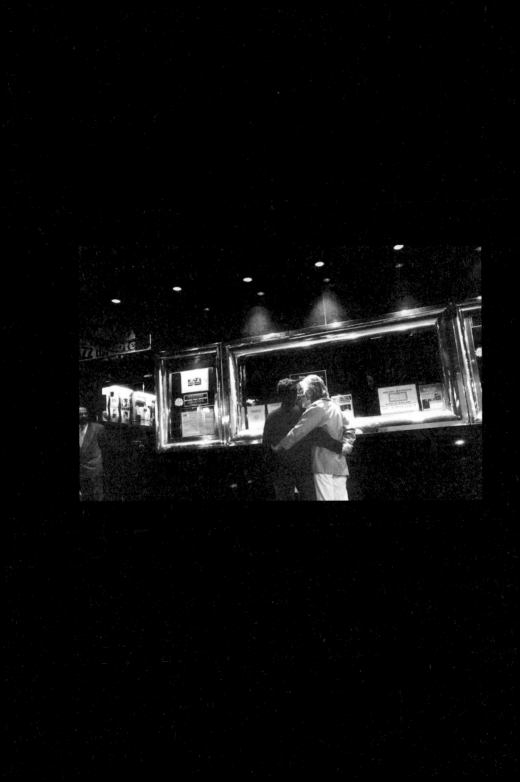

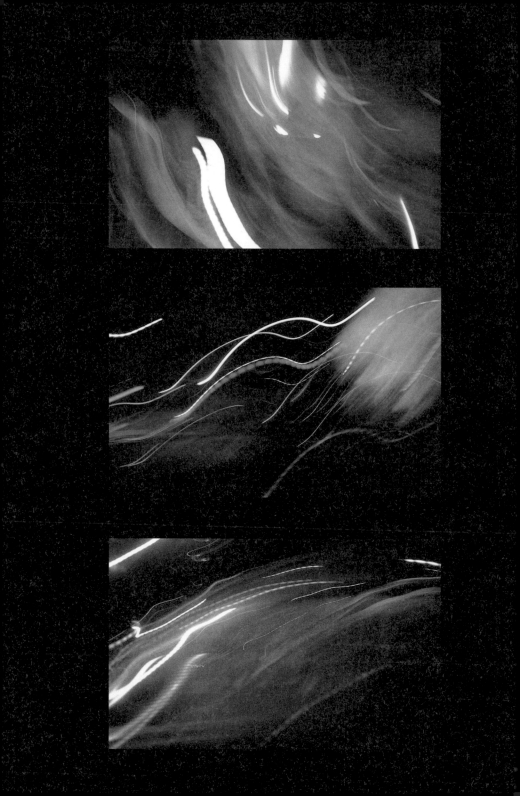

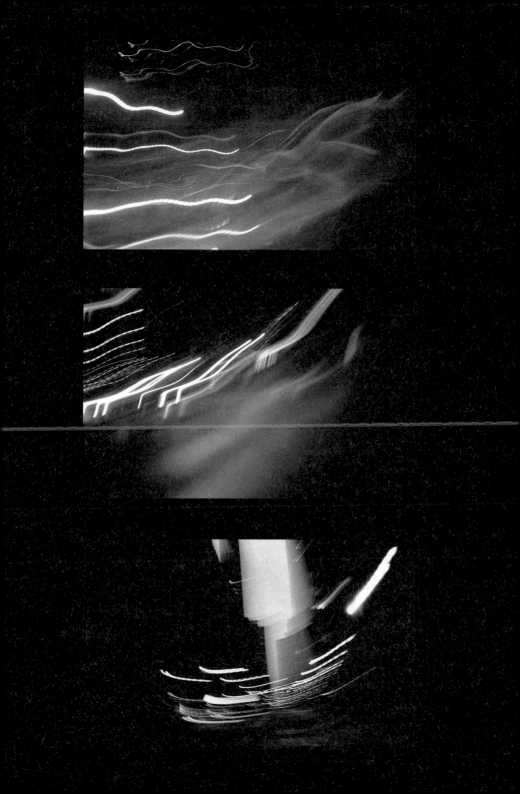

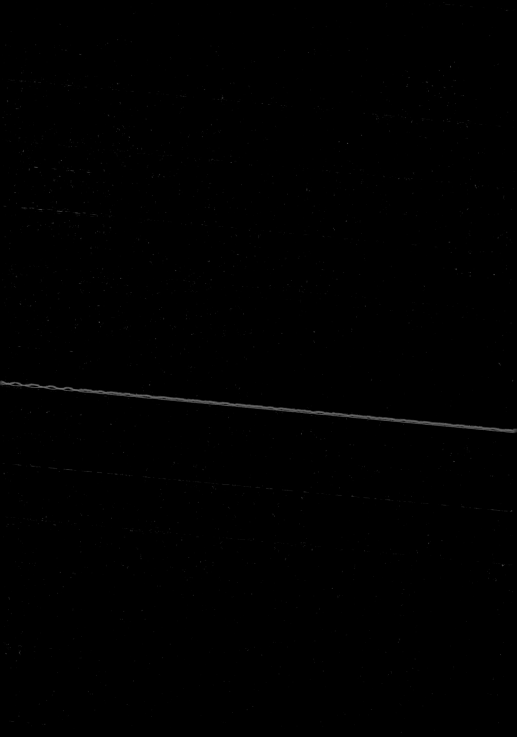

Back Seat Adventure
The New York Taxi Business and its Oddities

It was on 6 October 1998, at about 9.30 in the morning, that Mr Mohammad Rahman, resident on Ocean Parkway in Brooklyn, and previously occupied as an assistant in a restaurant, was proceeding in an easterly direction along 20th Street in his taxi.
At the level of Avenue of the Americas, his cab rammed a parked car. Instead of stopping, Mr Rahman put on a turn of speed and fled. In so doing, he hit a 22-year-old man from New Jersey, who was just about to cross the street. While the ambulance was taking care of the victim, one Aaron Smith, Mr Rahman was still on the road. The police only managed to stop him a short while later, but not before he had driven his taxi into another car parked at the roadside, this time on 19th Street at the corner of Park Avenue South. Mr Rahman had his license withdrawn that very same day. His first day as a taxi driver was also his last.

There are 40,592 drivers registered as working in public undertakings in New York. They drive all kinds of vehicles, from limousines to minibuses, through the skyscraper valleys of midtown, the maze of lanes downtown, or along the elegant boulevard of Broadway. The great majority, however, drive one of the 12,187 cabs licensed by the TLC, the Taxi & Limousine Commission. The streets of New York are characterized by these yellow Fords, known in the jargon as "Medallions". "Cabs and cabbies are the nerve network of the city," says David Bradford. Others, by contrast, regard them as more like a virus. However that might be, their reputation is imbued with myths and clichés. The joke – What's the difference between a London and a New York taxi driver? – is still the most harmless on the subject. The difference? A Londoner speaks English.

According to the *New York Times*, only 16% of all New York cab drivers in 1992 gave English as their mother tongue. Urdu had already climbed to 15%. Among the 100 remaining dialects and languages represented, those from the Indian subcontinent predominated, chiefly Punjabi and Bengali. Arabic was close on their heels. Most New York taxi drivers come from Asia and the Middle East, and many from Africa. "Their lives consist only of taxi, sleep and family" (Bradford). The stereotype image of the cabbie of the 1970s is today nothing but a hazy memory. The man behind the wheel of the yellow street cruiser used to have a growling Brooklyn accent (Hey, whaddaya doin' here?), and he knew every pothole in the asphalt and every dead end in town. Today in 1998, according to the *New York Times*, "...this relatively benign image had transmuted into Travis Bickle from the movie *Taxi Driver*: a sleep-deprived, psychotic loner with a schoolboy crush on Cybill Shepherd and an assassin's approach to politics."

Everyone has his own New York taxi driver horror story. Like the one about getting in at the Rockefeller Center to go to the World Trade Center. A 10-dollar trip. But it may be that the Russian cabbie takes a detour via the East Village and FDR Driveway along the East River, drives deliberately past the intended destination, in order to charge 16 dollars for this unwanted sightseeing tour. And passengers who make a critical comment can reckon with a string of insults.

All the city guides try to warn visitors – seriously or jokingly – about the oddities of the local taxi business. Take for example the collected laments of Jackie Mason and Raoul Felder in their *Survival Guide to New York City*. Quote: "Forget all the ugly things you have heard about the New York taxi situation. Taxis in New York present absolutely no problem to a prospective passenger – that is, unless the passenger wants to go somewhere in one of them."

Then there are problems. In this context, Mason and Felder pose a series of inevitable questions. Where do you find one? How do you persuade the driver to take you where you want to go? Why do cabbies always try to run pedestrians down? Why do they annoy their customers by playing oriental fertility chants? And why do they obviously find leaving someone standing in the rain more pleasurable than sex? Bizarre questions. Hop in, please.

And of course no one can understand that the overwhelming majority of New York taxi drivers find it totally impossible to give change for a 20-dollar bill. A cabbie needs three things: a cab, gas, and change. That the New York version of the species never has more than two of these things, Mason and Felder explain by saying they count on the passenger being in enough of a hurry to say, "Keep the change."

In fairness one could note that a few dollars too much would be a small price to pay for the piece of theater often served up in New York taxis. Turbaned pilots, many of them barefoot, in their radioed conversations with their fellows, often behave as though they are giving the orders for air-strikes. During Ramadan, Muslims steer their cabs through the rivers of steel glassy-eyed and faint with hunger. Africans explain the favorite traditions of the inhabitants of Burkina Faso to their clientele, and if you're lucky, you may even leave one of these exotic, sealed-off capsules with a valuable insight.

Taxi Driver Wisdom is a book containing a collection of sayings and philosophical thoughts from the mouths of cabbies. (E.g. "People are scared of people here while I'm not even scared of a tiger." Or: "The car, it drives itself. You just ask it to turn.") The editor of *Taxi Driver Wisdom*, Risa Mickenberg, writes, "Hey. An ashram costs 2,500 dollars a week, a psychiatrist 100 dollars an hour. An astrologist will run you between 50 and 100 dollars. Even 1-900-Hot-Talk adds up. But a cab ride is only 1.50 dollars for the first mile and 25 cents for each additional fifth of a mile... At first, it might seem a little strange to ask a person who can't even find the Holland Tunnel to give your life direction, but try it."

New York's mayor Rudolph W. Giuliani is less understanding in such matters. He presumed in the spring of 1998 that "there is not a great deal of public sympathy for taxi drivers." For a long time now, Giuliani has been waging a minor war against cabbies. He justifies it by their inconsiderate driving, statistics showing that between 1990 and 1996 there was a 59% increase in accidents resulting in personal injury. Mr Rahman is not an isolated instance. Taxi drivers are one reason why the city's tabloid newspapers need not fear a lack of material. As a rule it does not take too long before yet another yellow Medallion thunders over the sidewalk, or even through the glass front of a hotel to end up in the middle of the lobby.

Giuliani has therefore instructed the police to be ruthless in their distribution of tickets when cabbies contravene traffic regulations, obstruct the flow of traffic or other nonsense. Maximum penalty: 1,000 dollars per offense plus temporary withdrawal of license. A one-day cabbies' strike in the spring of 1998 was unable to prevent the police from taking harsh measures. One might ask, however, whether it is really necessary to impose a 100-dollar fine for a defective indicator light, or to punish cabbies for stopping more than 12 inches from the curb in order to set down passengers.

In order to obtain a license as a taxi driver, you must be at least 19 years old, have a driver's license issued by the states of New York, New Jersey or Connecticut, and be attested as medically fit by a doctor appointed by the TLC. The TLC takes the applicant's fingerprints and checks his police record. The application costs 62 dollars, the fingerprints 50 dollars. And otherwise? Oh yes... a course which used to last 40 hours, and now 80, in which applicants are instructed in the geography of the city, the traffic regulations, and civilized forms of social intercourse.

During this course the Taxi Riders' Bill of Rights is likely to crop up, a ten-point code designed to ensure the passenger pleasant and satisfactory service. According to this Bill of Rights, passengers are entitled to, among other things, the right to prescribe the route, a cabbie who knows every address in the five boroughs of New York, a friendly driver who speaks English, a driver who observes the traffic regulations, a clean passenger compartment and trunk, and the right to refuse a tip in case of dissatisfaction. Someone somewhere wrote that the New York cabbie who fulfilled these criteria should be displayed in the zoo, the species having long since become extinct.

What does Michael Higgins say to that? Michael Higgins says, "Drive a taxi in New York – you'll wish you had an ejector button to fling people out of the back seat. You just have no idea what kind of lunatics get into your cab each day, every day. People are high. People are drunk. People are throwing up. I wish I could put up a sign: Bean eaters must use mass transit." Higgins has been driving a taxi in New York for ten years, and together with others, was given space in an article in the *New York Times*, in which the situation was aired from the drivers' point of view. And from this point of view, the job looks like a penal measure. The cabbie as the hostage of savage, heartless assassins. Higgins once more: "Then there are the businessmen. They're tense, they're late. They don't want to hear that red means stop or U-turns are illegal. They have big mouths and they use their tongues like a whip. Day in, day out, you have to listen to their condescending crap: go this way, go that way. Well, shut the hell up!"

It's not an easy job, that much is clear. Cabbies have to work hard for little money. That's due to the policy of the numerous Medallion hire companies, who charge hefty rentals. On the other hand, one can have some sympathy with their position. The number of Medallions on the streets is regulated by the TLC, which last bought 144 yellow cabs in 1997. For a total of 35 million dollars. That makes an average price of 243,055 dollars per cab. And the owners pass the commercial pressure on to the drivers, whose situation is visibly worsening.

The consequence is that the New York taxi business is threatening to deteriorate into an area where the only ones who struggle to survive are those who can do nothing else. Taxi-hire operator Allen Kaplan says, "There are guys coming in saying, 'Allen, I don't know if I can continue.'" Mostly it's the veterans of the urban jungle, those cabbies who've caused the fewest accidents and know the city like the back of their hands. A TLC traffic-court judge says, "It'll be interesting to see who leaves the business and who comes in to replace them. I don't think it's going to be a higher-quality driver at all because nobody in their right mind would want to do this job."

At this point perhaps it would be appropriate to relate a short story by journalist Dan Rattinger, which describes an encounter of the special kind with a taxi driver named Muninul Purkaysiha. Rattinger got in and asked to be taken to the intersection of Fifth Avenue and 44th.

After a while, Mr Purkaysiha turned round and said, "Could you please give me directions, sir?"

Rattinger said once more, "Fifth and 44th." Only then did he realize that his cabbie didn't know how to get there.

Rattinger said, "Make a right and go over to Park, and then go down Park for a while."

"Park?" came the tentative reply.

Rattinger then lets the reader share the experience of how, in the ultimate metropolis, in which everything turns on street names and numbers, he had to learn to think once more as if he lived in the country. Because evidently his chauffeur came from the country, from some province at the end of the world. "In the city it's 75 Fifth Avenue, Apartment 3B, it's between 18th and 19th," writes Rattinger. But in his case, that didn't work any more. Everything was totally different. He had to describe the building, its size, its color. He provided Mr Purkaysiha with help on getting his bearings, so that he could find his way between the hooting trucks and buses to which he got dangerously near. And when they arrived, the driver said, "Yes sir."

Rattinger asked, "How long have you been in America?"

Muninul said, "Yes."

The fare was five dollars. Rattinger gave the cabbie a 10-dollar bill and said, "You can give me change of six." Muninul gave him five dollars back, and a receipt for $3376.25.

Rattinger's story ended with the sentence: "Good luck in America, Mr Purkaysiha."

Abenteuer Rücksitz
Das New Yorker Taxigewerbe und seine Kuriositäten

Es war am 6. Oktober 1998 gegen 9.30 Uhr, als Mr. Mohammad Rahman, wohnhaft
Ocean Parkway in Brooklyn und zuvor als Aushilfe in einem Restaurant tätig, mit
seinem Taxi auf der 20th Street in östliche Richtung fuhr. In Höhe der Avenue of the
Americas rammte der Wagen ein parkendes Auto. Anstatt anzuhalten und auszusteigen,
gab Mr. Rahman ordentlich Gas und flüchtete. Dabei erfaßte sein Gefährt einen 22jähri-
gen Mann aus New Jersey, der gerade die Straße überqueren wollte. Während sich die
Ambulanz bereits um das Opfer namens Aaron Smith kümmerte, war Mr. Rahman noch
immer unterwegs. Die Polizei konnte ihn erst kurz darauf stellen. Inzwischen hatte er
sein Fahrzeug an der 19th Street, Ecke Park Avenue South in einen weiteren am
Straßenrand abgestellten Pkw gesteuert. Mr. Rahman wurde noch am selben Tag die
Lizenz entzogen. Sein erster Arbeitstag als Taxifahrer war auch sein letzter.

40 592 in privaten Fuhrunternehmen tätige Chauffeure sind in New York City registriert.
Sie steuern allerlei Karossen, Limousinen und Kleinbusse durch die Häuserschluchten
Midtowns, die verwinkelten Gassen von Downtown oder über den erhabenen Broadway.
Die überwiegende Mehrzahl jedoch fährt eines der 12 187 von der Taxi & Limousine
Commission (TLC) zugelassenen Cabs. Diese gelb lackierten Fabrikate des Automobilher-
stellers Ford, im Branchenjargon „Medallions" genannt, prägen die Straßen New Yorks.
„Cabs und Cabbies sind das Nervengeflecht der Stadt", sagt David Bradford. Andere
halten sie allerdings mehr für einen Virus, um im Bild zu bleiben. Jedenfalls ist ihr Ruf

von Mythen und Klischees durchzogen. Wobei der Witz, was einen Londoner von einem New Yorker Taxifahrer unterscheide, noch die harmloseste Anekdote in diesem Zusammenhang ist. Was einen Londoner von einem New Yorker Cabbie unterscheidet? Der Londoner spricht Englisch.

Laut der *New York Times* gaben 1992 lediglich 16 Prozent aller New Yorker Taxifahrer Englisch als Muttersprache an. Urdu brachte es zur gleichen Zeit schon auf 15 Prozent. Unter den verbliebenen 100 Dialekten und Sprachen, die insgesamt gezählt wurden, überwogen Idiome vom indischen Subkontinent, vorweg Punjabi und Bengali. Gleich dahinter rangierte Arabisch. Die meisten Taxifahrer in New York kommen aus Asien und dem Nahen Osten, ein großer Teil aus Afrika. „Ihr Leben besteht nur aus Taxi, Schlafen und Familie" (Bradford). Das stereotype Bild des Cabbies aus den 70er Jahren ist heute nur noch eine verschwommene Erinnerung. Früher handelte es sich bei dem Fahrer des gelben Straßenkreuzers meistens um einen mit Brooklyner Akzent (Hey, whaddaya doin' here?) grummelnden Mann, der jedes Loch im Straßenbelag und jede Sackgasse in der Stadt kannte. Heute, so die *New York Times* 1998, „hat sich dieses Image verwandelt in Travis Bickle aus dem Film *Taxi Driver*, einen übernächtigten, psychotischen Einzelgänger mit der Herangehensweise eines Attentäters." Jeder hat seine eigene Horrorgeschichte über eine New Yorker Taxifahrt parat. Eine Story etwa, bei der man in der Fifth Avenue am Rockefeller Center einsteigt und zum World Trade Center will. Ein 10-Dollar-Trip. Doch dann kann es passieren, daß der russische Fahrer einen Umweg über das East Village und den FDR-Driveway entlang des East River nimmt, absichtlich am anvisierten Ziel vorbeifährt, um am Ende dieser nicht bestellten Stadtrundfahrt 16 Dollar kassieren zu wollen. Und sollte der Fahrgast eine kritische Bemerkung vorbringen, hat er mit diversen Beleidigungen zu rechnen.

Alle Stadtführer versuchen mit ernsthaften Warnungen oder kernigen Späßen auf die Kuriositäten des hiesigen Taxigewerbes aufmerksam zu machen. Da wären etwa die gesammelten Klagen von Jackie Mason und Raoul Felder in ihrem *Survival Guide to New York City*. Zitat: „Vergessen Sie all die häßlichen Dinge, die Sie über die Situation in New York gehört haben. Taxis stellen in dieser Stadt absolut kein Problem dar, es sei denn, man möchte in einem von ihnen irgendwo hingebracht werden."
Dann gibt es Ärger. Mason und Felder stellen in diesem Zusammenhang auch gleich eine Reihe unvermeidlicher Fragen. Wie findet man eines? Wie bewegt man den Fahrer dazu, einen dorthin zu bringen, wohin man möchte? Wieso versuchen Cabbies, alle Fußgänger umzufahren? Warum belästigen sie ihre Kundschaft mit dem Abspielen fernöstlicher Fruchtbarkeitsgesänge? Und warum macht ihnen, einen Menschen im Regen stehen zu lassen, offensichtlich mehr Spaß als Sex? Bizarre Fragen. Bitte einsteigen.

Und natürlich kann niemand verstehen, daß es der überwiegenden Anzahl New Yorker Taxifahrer nicht möglich ist, in US-Währung auf einen 20-Dollar-Schein herauszugeben.

Drei Dinge braucht ein Cabbie: ein Taxi, Benzin und Wechselgeld. Daß die New Yorker Version der Spezies immer nur zwei Dinge dabei hat, erklären sich Mason und Felder damit, daß sie wohl damit rechnen, der Fahrgast sei in Eile und werde sagen: „Behalten Sie den Rest."

Der Fairneß halber könnte man jetzt allerdings anmerken, daß ein paar Dollar zuviel immer noch ein bescheidener Obolus wären für das Schauspiel, das einem in New Yorker Taxis oft geboten wird. Turban tragende Fahrer, manche davon barfuß, verhalten sich beim Funkverkehr mit Kollegen als gäben sie Kommandos für Bombenattacken; Muslime steuern ihr Gefährt während des Ramadans mit glasigen Augen und vor Hunger der Ohnmacht nahe durch Blechlawinen; Afrikaner erklären ihrer Kundschaft die bevorzugten Traditionen der Bewohner von Burkina Faso, und wenn man Glück hat, verläßt man diese exotischen, vom Rest der Welt abgeschlossenen Kapseln sogar mit einer kostbaren Erkenntnis.

Taxi Driver Wisdom ist ein Buch mit einer Sammlung von Sinnsprüchen und philosophischen Gedanken von Cabbies (z.B. „Hier haben die Menschen vor anderen Menschen Angst, dabei habe ich nicht mal Angst vor einem Tiger" und „Der Wagen fährt von alleine, du bittest ihn nur, abzubiegen"). Der Herausgeber von *Taxi Driver Wisdom*, Risa Mickenberg, schreibt: „Hey, ein Ashram kostet 2500 Dollar pro Woche, ein Psychiater 100 Dollar in der Stunde und ein Astrologe macht zwischen 50 und 100 Dollar. Eine Taxifahrt ist billiger. Anfangs mag es verrückt erscheinen, jemandem, der nicht mal den Holland Tunnel findet, richtungsweisende Fragen über das Leben zu stellen, aber es lohnt sich."

New Yorks Bürgermeister Rudolph W. Giuliani hat für so etwas weniger Verständnis. Der mutmaßte im Frühjahr 1998: „Für Taxifahrer gibt es hier keine großartige öffentliche Sympathie." Giuliani führt seit längerem einen Kleinkrieg gegen Cabbies. Er begründet dies mit dem rücksichtslosen Fahrverhalten der Fahrer, von dem statistisch belegt ist, daß es zwischen 1990 und 1996 zu einer 59%igen Steigerung von Unfällen mit Verletzungsfolge geführt hat. Mr. Rahman ist da kein Einzelfall. Taxifahrer sind ein Grund, warum die Boulevardzeitungen der Stadt nicht fürchten müssen, daß ihnen der Stoff ausgeht. Es dauert in aller Regel nicht allzu lange, bis ein gelbes Medallion mal wieder übers Trottoir oder sogar durch die Glasfront eines Hotels bis mitten in die Lobby donnert.

Giuliani hat daher die Polizei angewiesen, rücksichtslos Strafzettel zu verteilen, wenn Cabbies Verkehrsregeln mißachten, den Verkehrsfluß hemmen oder sonstwie Blödsinn anstellen. Maximale Strafe: 1000 Dollar pro Vergehen plus zeitweisem Entzug der Taxilizenz. Ein eintägiger Streik der Cabbies im Frühjahr 1998 konnte nichts daran ändern, daß die Ordnungshüter inzwischen hart durchgreifen. Wobei sich allerdings die Frage stellt, ob es tatsächlich nötig ist, für ein kaputtes Blinklicht 100 Dollar Strafe zu verhängen und Cabbies zu züchtigen, weil sie weiter als zwölf Inches vom Randstein entfernt stehenblieben, um Fahrgäste aussteigen zu lassen.

Um in New York eine Lizenz als Taxifahrer zu erhalten, muß man mindestens 19 Jahre alt, im Besitz einer Fahrerlaubnis der US-Bundesstaaten New York, New Jersey oder Connecticut und medizinisch fit sein, was von einem Amtsarzt der TLC überprüft wird. Die TLC nimmt außerdem die Fingerabdrücke des Antragstellers und checkt sein polizeiliches Führungszeugnis. Der Antrag kostet 62 Dollar, die Fingerabdrücke 50 Dollar. Und sonst? Ach ja, es gibt da noch einen Kurs, der früher mal 40 Stunden dauerte, inzwischen 80 Stunden, und in dem die Bewerber über die Geographie der Stadt, die Verkehrsregeln und zivilisierte Umgangsformen aufgeklärt werden.

Dabei kommt wohl auch die Taxi Rider's Bill of Rights zur Sprache, die mit ihren zehn Punkten dem Fahrgast einen angenehmen und zufriedenstellenden Service garantieren soll. Es stehen ihm laut dieser Bill of Rights u.a. zu: das Recht, die Route vorzugeben; ein Cabbie, der jede Adresse in den fünf Boroughs von New York kennt; ein freundlicher, Englisch sprechender Fahrer; ein die Verkehrsregeln beachtender Fahrer; ein sauberer Fahrgast- sowie Kofferraum plus das Recht, das Trinkgeld zu verweigern, sollte der Kunde unzufrieden sein. Irgendwo hat mal jemand geschrieben, man sollte das New Yorker Cabbie-Exemplar, das all dem entspricht, im Zoo ausstellen. Die Sorte sei nämlich längst ausgestorben.

Was sagt Michael Higgins dazu? Michael Higgins sagt: „Taxifahren in New York? Du wünschst dir, du hättest einen Knopf für einen Schleudersitz auf der Rückbank. Du hast gar keine Ahnung, welche Art von Wahnsinnigen du jeden Tag im Auto hast. Die Leute sind auf Drogen. Die Leute sind besoffen. Die Leute kotzen, sie stinken. Manchmal würde ich gerne ein Schild mit der Aufschrift anbringen: Bohnenliebhaber müssen die öffentlichen Verkehrsmittel benutzen." Higgins fährt seit zehn Jahren Taxi und kam zusammen mit anderen Kollegen in einem Artikel der *New York Times* zu Wort, in dem die Situation aus der Sicht der Fahrer beleuchtet wurde. Und aus dieser Perspektive stellt sich der Job dar wie eine Art Strafarbeit. Der Cabbie als Geisel wildgewordener, herzloser Attentäter. Higgins: „Da gibt es dann noch die Geschäftsleute. Sie sind nervös. Sie sind spät dran. Sie wollen nicht hören, daß Rot Halt bedeutet und U-Turns illegal sind. Sie haben eine große Klappe und benutzen ihre Zunge wie eine Peitsche. Tagein, tagaus muß man sich ihren herablassenden Mist anhören: ‚Nimm' diesen Weg, nimm' jenen Weg. Well, die sollen die Luft anhalten!' "

Es ist kein leichter Job, soviel steht fest. Cabbies müssen für wenig Geld hart arbeiten. Das liegt an der Strategie der zahlreichen Medallion-Verleiher, die ihre Vehikel gegen üppige Gebühren vermieten. Andererseits ist deren Haltung nicht ganz unverständlich. Die Anzahl der Medallions auf den Straßen wird von der TLC reguliert. Diese hat 1997 letztmalig 144 gelbe Droschken mit Taxilizenz für insgesamt 35 Millionen Dollar gekauft. Das ergibt einen Durchschnittspreis von 243 055 Dollar pro Cab, auf deren Zulassung die TLC ein Monopol hat. Und die Taxiunternehmen geben diesen Druck an die Fahrer weiter, deren wirtschaftliche Situation sich zusehends verschlechtert.

Die Konsequenz: Das New Yorker Taxigewerbe droht zu einem Bereich zu verkommen, in dem nur noch jene ums Überleben kämpfen, denen keine andere Möglichkeit bleibt. Taxiverleiher Allen Kaplan sagt: „Es kommen immer wieder Jungs zu mir, die sagen: ‚Allen, ich weiß nicht, ob ich weitermachen kann.'" Meistens handelt es sich dabei um die Veteranen des Großstadtdschungels, jene Cabbies, die die wenigsten Unfälle bauen und den Stadtplan intus haben. Ein Richter am TLC Verkehrsgericht meint: „Es wird interessant sein zu sehen, wer diese Leute ersetzen wird. Ich glaube nicht, daß es sich dabei um besser qualifizierte Fahrer handelt, denn wer macht diesen Job denn noch, wenn er alle Tassen im Schrank hat?"

Dazu paßt vielleicht eine Kurzgeschichte des Publizisten Dan Rattinger, der darin eine Begegnung der besonderen Art mit einem Taxifahrer namens Muninul Purkaysiha schildert. Rattinger stieg also ein und verlangte, zur Kreuzung Fifth Avenue und 44th gebracht zu werden.
Nach einer Weile, drehte sich Mr. Purkaysiha um und sagte: „Könnten Sie mir bitte Anweisungen geben."
Rattinger sagte erneut: „Fifth und 44th." Erst dann verstand er. Sein Cabbie wußte nicht, wie man dorthin kommt.
Rattinger sagte: „Biegen Sie rechts ab und rüber zur Park Avenue, danach eine Weile die Park runter."
„Park?", kam es zögernd zurück.
Rattinger läßt den Leser anschließend daran teilhaben, wie er in der ultimativen Metropolis, in der sich alles nach Straßennamen und Zahlen richtet, wieder lernen mußte, wie auf dem Land zu denken. Denn offensichtlich kam sein Chauffeur vom Land, aus irgendeiner Provinz am Ende der Welt. „In der Stadt heißt es 75 Fifth Avenue, zwischen 18th und 19th", schreibt Rattinger. Doch das funktionierte in seinem Fall nicht mehr. Jetzt war alles völlig anders. Er mußte die Gebäude beschreiben, ihre Größe, ihre Farbe, er gab Orientierungshilfen, damit Mr. Purkaysiha sich zwischen hupenden Last- wagen und Bussen, denen er gefährlich nahe kam, zurechtfinden konnte. Als sie anka- men, sagte der Fahrer: „Yes, Sir."
Rattinger fragte: „Wie lange sind sie schon in Amerika?"
Muninul sagte: „Yes."
Die Taxe betrug 5 Dollar. Rattinger gab dem Cabbie einen 10-Dollar-Schein und sagte: „Geben Sie mir auf 6 Dollar raus." Muninul gab ihm 5 Dollar zurück, ließ eine Quittung ausdrucken und auf der stand $3376,25.
Rattingers Geschichte endet mit dem Satz: „Viel Glück in Amerika, Mr. Purkaysiha."

L'aventure sur la banquette arrière
Le chauffeur de taxi new-yorkais et les curiosités de son travail

Il était environ 9 heures 30, le matin du 6 octobre 1998, lorsque M. Mohammad Rahman, domicilié Ocean Parkway à Brooklyn, ancien plongeur de restaurant de son état, parcourait au volant de son taxi la 20e Rue en direction de l'Est. À hauteur de l'Avenue of the Americas, sa voiture percuta une automobile en stationnement. Au lieu de s'arrêter et de descendre de son véhicule, M. Rahman accéléra à fond et prit la poudre d'escampette. Dans sa fuite, il renversa un jeune homme de 22 ans, originaire du New Jersey, qui traversait fortuitement la chaussée à ce moment-là. Pendant que l'ambulance s'occupait d'Aaron Smith, la victime, M. Rahman continuait de sillonner la ville. La police ne parvint à l'arrêter qu'un peu plus tard. Entre-temps, sa voiture en avait encore percuté une autre, garée au bord de la route, au carrefour de la 19e Rue et de Park Avenue Sud. M. Rahman a dû restituer sa licence le jour même. Son premier jour de travail comme chauffeur de taxi fut aussi son dernier.

40 592 chauffeurs travaillant pour des entreprises privées sont enregistrés à New York City. Ils conduisent toutes sortes de voitures, des limousines aux minibus, à travers les artères de Midtown, les ruelles tortueuses de Downtown ou sur la prestigieuse Broadway. La très grande majorité conduit cependant l'un des 12 187 « cabs » agréés par la Taxi & Limousine Commission (TLC). Ces voitures jaunes, toutes fabriquées par Ford et que les initiés surnomment « Medallions », sont indissociables du paysage urbain de New York. « Cabs et cabbies sont le système nerveux de la ville », dit David Bradford.

D'autres y verraient plutôt – pour cultiver la métaphore – un virus. Quoi qu'il en soit, leur légende est constellée de mythes et de clichés. Et encore la blague sur ce qui fait la différence entre un chauffeur de taxi londonien et son homologue new-yorkais est-elle la plaisanterie la plus anodine à ce sujet. Mais, au fait, connaissez-vous la différence entre un cabbie londonien et un cabbie new-yorkais ? Le Londonien parle anglais.

Selon le *New York Times*, en 1992, 16 % seulement des conducteurs de taxi new-yorkais ont déclaré avoir l'anglais pour langue maternelle. Cette année là, le taux de l'ourdou était déjà de 15 %. Parmi les cent autres langues et dialectes répertoriés au total, ce sont les idiomes du sous-continent indien, en particulier le punjabi et le bengali, qui prédominaient. Talonnés par l'arabe. La majorité des conducteurs de taxi de New York viennent d'Asie et du Proche-Orient, une grande partie, d'Afrique. « Leur vie tourne autour de trois piliers seulement : taxi, dormir et famille » (dixit Bradford). Aujourd'hui, le cliché stéréotype du cabbie des années 70 n'est plus qu'un vague souvenir. Jadis, l'homme coincé derrière le volant de l'imposante voiture jaune était le plus souvent un homme qui grommelait avec son accent de Brooklyn (Hey, whaddaya doin' here?) et qui connaissait le moindre enfoncement de la chaussée, la moindre impasse de la ville. Aujourd'hui, en 1998, déclarait le *New York Times*, « ce cliché a fait place à Travis Bickle du film *Taxi Driver*, un solitaire psychopathe, insomniaque, au profil d'assassin. »

Tout le monde peut vous raconter à brûle-pourpoint une histoire à faire frémir concernant une course en taxi new-yorkais. Une histoire comme celle où l'on monte par exemple dans un taxi sur la Cinquième Avenue, à hauteur du Rockefeller Center, pour se rendre au World Trade Center. Un trajet de 10 dollars. Et pourtant, il peut arriver que le conducteur russe vous fasse faire un détour par East Village et le FDR-Driveway le long de l'East River, passant intentionnellement à côté de la destination souhaitée pour, à la fin de cette excursion en ville évidemment contrainte et forcée, vouloir encaisser 16 dollars. Et que le passager ne s'avise pas de lui faire une critique sous peine d'être traité de tous les noms d'oiseaux.

Tous les guides touristiques attirent votre attention par de sérieuses mises en garde ou de plaisanteries sur les curiosités du métier de chauffeur de taxi dans cette ville. Nous pourrions citer par exemple le recueil de plaintes de Jackie Mason et Raoul Felder dans leur *Survival Guide to New York City*. Citation : « Oubliez toutes les choses horribles que l'on vous a racontées sur la situation à New York. Les taxis ne posent aucun problème dans cette ville, sauf si vous souhaitez, à bord de l'un d'eux, être conduit à un endroit précis. » C'est alors que les ennuis commencent. Dans ce contexte, Mason et Felder posent aussi, dans la foulée, toute une série de questions inévitables. Comment trouver un taxi ? Comment convaincre le chauffeur de vraiment vous amener là où vous souhaitez vous rendre ? Pourquoi les cabbies cherchent-ils à écraser tous les piétons ? Pourquoi cassentils les oreilles de leurs clients en passant des cassettes de musique extrême-orientale censée favoriser la fécondité ? Et pourquoi prennent-ils manifestement plus de plaisir à laisser un piéton sous la pluie qu'à faire l'amour ? Questions pour le moins bizarres. Mais prenez donc place !

Et, naturellement, personne ne peut vraiment comprendre que la très grande majorité des chauffeurs de taxi new-yorkais soit dans l'impossibilité de rendre la monnaie en argent américain sur un billet de banque américain de 20 dollars. Un cabbie a besoin de trois choses : un taxi, de l'essence et de la monnaie. Le spécimen new-yorkais n'a toujours que deux choses sur lui, fait sans doute dû, comme le croient Mason et Felder, à ce qu'ils s'attendent à ce que le client soit pressé et rétorque : « Gardez la monnaie ! »

Mais, par loyauté, il faut toutefois préciser que quelques dollars de trop sont encore une modeste obole vu le spectacle que les taxis de New York vous offrent fréquemment. Des chauffeurs en turban, certains pieds nus, envoient des messages radio à leurs collègues comme s'ils dirigeaient une attaque à la bombe ; pendant le ramadan, des musulmans aux yeux vitreux, au bord de la syncope tant ils sont affamés, se faufilent à l'aveuglette à travers les embouteillages ; des Africains expliquent à leur clientèle les traditions préférées des habitants du Burkina Faso et, avec un peu de chance, on quitte même ces capsules exotiques coupées du reste du monde, riche d'un enseignement précieux.

Taxi Driver Wisdom est un recueil des sentences et des réflexions philosophiques des cabbies (par exemple « Ici, les hommes ont peur de leurs semblables, alors que moi je n'ai pas même peur d'un tigre. » et « La voiture roule toute seule, il suffit de la prier de tourner à l'angle. »). L'éditeur de *Taxi Driver Wisdom*, Risa Mickenberg, écrit : « Hey, un ashram coûte 2 500 dollars par semaine, un psychiatre 100 dollars de l'heure et un astrologue facture entre 50 et 100 dollars. Un trajet en taxi coûte beaucoup moins cher. Au début, il peut paraître absurde de poser des questions sur le sens de la vie à quelqu'un qui ne trouve même pas l'entrée du Holland Tunnel, mais cela en vaut la peine. »

Rudolph W. Giuliani, le maire de New York, n'a pas vraiment d'indulgence pour ce genre de choses. N'a-t-il pas déclaré, au printemps 1998 : « Les New Yorkais n'éprouvent pas de sympathie particulière à l'égard des chauffeurs de taxi. » Il y a longtemps déjà que Giuliani se bat contre les cabbies. Ce qu'il justifie par le comportement sans scrupules des chauffeurs qui, entre 1990 et 1996, à en croire les statistiques, ont été responsables d'une augmentation de 59 % du nombre des accidents avec blessés. M. Rahman n'est donc pas une exception. Les chauffeurs de taxi font en sorte que les tabloïds de la ville ne seront jamais à court de nouvelles sensationnelles. En règle générale, il ne faut pas attendre trop longtemps pour qu'un Medallion jaune fonce une fois de plus sur le trottoir ou se retrouve dans l'entrée d'un hôtel après avoir réduit en miettes sa façade de verre.

Giuliani a donc donné l'ordre à la police d'être impitoyable envers les cabbies qui ne respectent pas le code de la route, entravent la circulation ou font une bêtise quelconque. Amende maximum : 1 000 dollars par infraction, plus retrait temporaire de la licence de chauffeur de taxi. Une grève d'une journée des cabbies, au printemps 1998, n'a rien pu y changer et les gardiens de la paix continuent de sévir d'une main de fer. On peut toutefois se demander s'il est vraiment nécessaire d'infliger une amende de 100 dollars pour un clignotant cassé et de vouloir éduquer les cabbies sous prétexte qu'ils se garent à plus de 12 pouces de la bordure du trottoir pour faire descendre leurs passagers.

Pour obtenir une licence de chauffeur de taxi à New York, il faut avoir au moins 19 ans, posséder un permis de conduire des États fédérés américains de New York, du New Jersey ou du Connecticut et être en bonne condition physique, ce qui est contrôlé par un médecin officiel de la TLC. De plus, la TLC prélève les empreintes digitales du candidat et vérifie son casier judiciaire. La demande coûte 62 dollars, plus 50 dollars pour les empreintes digitales. Et à part ça ? Ah oui, il y a encore un cours, qui durait jadis 40 heures contre 80 heures maintenant, durant lequel les aspirants à la licence doivent apprendre la géographie de la ville, le code de la route et des règles de comportement civilisé.

À cette occasion, on évoque sans aucun doute aussi la déclaration des droits des clients de taxi, le Bill of Rights of Taxi Riders, qui, avec ses dix points, est censée garantir au passager un service agréable et satisfaisant. Selon cette déclaration, le passager a un certain nombre de droits : le droit d'indiquer le trajet à suivre ; d'avoir un cabbie qui connaît chaque adresse dans les cinq boroughs de New York ; un conducteur aimable et parlant anglais, un conducteur respectueux du code de la route, un habitacle et un coffre propres, plus le droit de refuser de donner un pourboire lorsqu'il est mécontent. Un jour, quelqu'un a écrit que l'on devrait exposer dans un zoo un exemplaire de cabbie new-yorkais remplissant toutes ces conditions. Selon lui, cette espèce serait en effet éteinte depuis longtemps.

Que dit à ce sujet Michael Higgins ? Eh bien, Michael Higgins rétorque : « Conduire un taxi à New York ? Tu souhaiterais avoir un bouton qui actionne un siège éjectable intégré à la banquette arrière. On ne s'imagine pas quel genre de dingues on transporte chaque jour dans sa voiture. Les uns sont dopés à mort. D'autres sont complètement bourrés. Les gens dégueulent, ils puent. Quelquefois, j'aimerais avoir un panonceau avec la mention : « les amateurs de haricots sont priés de prendre les transports en commun ». Higgins est chauffeur de taxi depuis dix ans et, avec quelques-uns de ses collègues, il a, un jour, pris la parole dans un article du *New York Times* qui décrivait la situation du point de vue des chauffeurs. Et, à leurs yeux, ce boulot est une variante de la peine de travaux forcés. Le cabbie, otage de terroristes sauvages et impitoyables.

Mais, selon Higgins : «Il ne faut pas oublier les hommes d'affaires. Ils sont nerveux. Ils sont en retard. Ils refusent d'accepter que l'on doit s'arrêter au feu rouge et que les demi-tours inopinés sont interdits. Ils ont une grande gueule et se servent de leur langue comme d'un fouet. Du matin au soir, il faut les entendre raconter leurs conneries : « Prends ce chemin-ci, prends ce chemin-là. Mais qu'ils la bouclent un peu à la fin ! »

Ce n'est pas un boulot facile, cela, au moins, c'est sûr. Les cabbies doivent travailler dur pour gagner trois fois rien. C'est le résultat de la politique que mènent les nombreux loueurs de Medallion, qui cèdent leurs véhicules contre une somme exorbitante. D'un autre côté, il faut comprendre leur situation. C'est la TLC qui règle le nombre de Medallions circulant dans les rues. En 1997, celle-ci a vendu pour la dernière fois 144 taxis jaunes pour une somme totale de 35 millions de dollars. Soit une moyenne de 24 3055 dollars par cab. Et leurs propriétaires répercutent la pression commerciale sur leurs chauffeurs, dont la situation se dégrade à vue d'œil.

Conséquence : le métier de chauffeur de taxi à New York risque de se dégrader et de devenir l'activité de ceux qui, pour survivre, n'ont aucune autre alternative. Un loueur de taxis, Allen Kaplan, a ainsi déclaré un jour : « Il y a de plus en plus de types qui viennent me voir et disent : « Allen, je ne sais pas si je peux continuer. » Le plus souvent, il s'agit en l'occurrence des vétérans dans cette jungle métropolitaine, de ces cabbies qui causent le moins d'accidents et connaissent le plan de la ville comme leur poche. Un juge du tribunal de la circulation de la TLC déclare, prémonitoire : « Il sera intéressant de voir qui va remplacer ces gens-là. Je ne pense pas qu'il s'agisse de chauffeurs plus qualifiés, car qui voudra encore faire un tel boulot s'il est vraiment sain d'esprit. »

Il serait peut-être judicieux d'illustrer ce point de vue par une anecdote relatée par le journaliste Dan Rattinger, qui a fait un jour une rencontre d'un genre particulier avec un chauffeur de taxi du nom de Muninul Purkaysiha. Rattinger a donc pris un taxi et demandé au chauffeur de l'amener au carrefour de la Cinquième Avenue et de la 44e. Au bout d'un certain temps, M. Purkaysiha s'est retourné et lui a demandé : « Vous voudriez bien me donner des instructions ? »
Rattinger a donc répété : « Cinquième et 44e. » C'est alors seulement qu'il a compris. Son cabbie ignorait la route à prendre.
Rattinger lui a dit : « Tournez à droite et prenez Park Avenue, puis longez le parc pendant un moment. »
« Parc ? » s'est-il entendu demander avec hésitation.
Rattinger fait ensuite participer le lecteur aux efforts qu'il fait pour réapprendre à penser comme quelqu'un de la campagne alors que les deux hommes se trouvent dans la métropole par excellence, une ville où on ne s'exprime qu'en noms de rues et en

chiffres. En effet, son chauffeur venait apparemment de la campagne, d'une province quelconque à l'autre bout du monde. « En ville, on dit 75, Cinquième Avenue, c'est entre la 18ᵉ et la 19ᵉ », écrit Rattinger. Mais, dans son cas, le déclic ne se produisait plus. Maintenant, tout était complètement différent. Il lui fallut décrire les bâtiments, leur taille, leur couleur, donner au chauffeur des conseils pour l'aider à s'orienter, ce M. Purkaysiha qui slalomait entre les camions et bus, klaxonnant lorsqu'il se rapprochait dangereusement d'eux. Une fois arrivés, le chauffeur lança : « Yes, Sir. » Rattinger lui demanda : « Depuis combien de temps êtes-vous déjà en Amérique ? » Muninul répondit : « Yes. »

Le prix du trajet était de 5 dollars. Rattinger donna au cabbie un billet de dix dollars et lui dit : « Rendez-moi 4 dollars. » Muninul lui rendit 5 dollars, et lui tendit un reçu de 3 376,25 dollars.

L'histoire de Rattinger se termine par la phrase : « Bonne chance en Amérique, M. Purkaysiha. »

Another Day

The Restlessness of the Hunter
David Bradford on his Job as Cabbie

Sometimes you wonder how a flock of birds apparently fly higgledy-piggledy across each other without colliding. How? Because they fly along fixed paths. The same is true of cars in New York. How can so many of them drive across each other's paths in such a hectic fashion and so fast, without slamming together? Every car, too, has its invisible zone of sovereignty which is respected by every other. Taxi driving in New York is not so dangerous as it might seem at first sight.

And yet when I get into the car in the morning, I feel as if I were going to take part in a car race the whole day. Some taxi drivers do anything to get a fare. They cut straight across the roadway, or turn right from the left-hand lane. They break the speed limit. They cross the center line. They do U-turns. They do everything they're allowed to do and everything they're not allowed to do. Out there, they're your rivals, all of them. It's not like football, where you pass the ball to the man in the same colors. Here, every yellow car's a competitor. As a New York taxi driver, basically you have no friends on the road. The only friend you have is yourself.

I am a hunter. Cabbies are hunters. You're hungry when you don't have a fare, and every fare is a little rush. If you can't catch anyone for a while, you get nervous. Thirty-five minutes without a fare, jeez! You think of all the money you have to earn.

What, an hour without a fare, again!? You begin to doubt the color of your car. Is it really yellow? Then it happens. There is someone hailing just ahead and you are one of the three cabs at a redlight. Bang – you've played the lights just right and scored the fare.

You have to be clever in this business. A skillful driver, observant, psychologically strong. You have to have the street ahead in your sights, as well as the situation in your rear mirror. Your behavior is dependent on that of your competitors. You have to lose the other taxis, you stay in the center lane until you have to make a decision. In heavy traffic, it's always a minor existential question whether you keep right or left. Where are the most people? How do you get ahead quickest? I know the rhythm of every traffic light in the city. I know what time of day people are standing where.

120 dollars clear is the maximum, tips included. That's a good day's work. A real bad day could be 30 dollars. On average, a New York cabbie makes 70 to 80 dollars a day. That means at best a week's wages of 500 dollars for 11 or 12 hours work a day, six days a week. The situation for us here used to be better. The car-rental firm and the driver used to split the takings 51 to 49. Now, the garages charge horrific commissions for letting you drive their cars. 110 or 120 dollars a day is nothing unusual. The weekly rate could be 625 or sometimes even 650 dollars. Anyone who has to drive a taxi for the money is a poor sucker. Certainly, you won't gather much moss.

What you will gather is any amount of grotesque experience. Recently a guy got in and gave me seven instructions on how to get to his destination. I said, "Okay, I can remember half of them." Some people are intolerable. They think they've driven the route more often than anyone else. How often do they think I've driven every route already? Okay, the guy gets ratty, starts arguing with me, and when he gets out, he says, "And by the way, you're a pretty mediocre photographer too." That was wicked. But I thought, "Just you wait, one of these days I'll have my book." It also happens that you'll be sworn at for just about anything by anybody with an axe to grind. Some people spit at taxi drivers simply because they can't stand taxi drivers. These are people outside the cab I'm talking about.

Some days, it all comes together. You're brutally forced off the road, someone steals a fare from under your nose, you just miss having an accident, it's hot, you get stuck in a jam because a garbage truck is maneuvering in a narrow street, emptying the trashcans in slow motion. And if a timid car driver in front of you doesn't trust himself to weave past, you're stuck for half an hour between two blocks. That can ruin your day. You hardly make any dough, you waste a huge amount of time, and your morale takes a dive. At times like that, the car seems like your personal prison. Not to mention tickets. Sometimes you get two tickets for the same offense, one from the TLC, the other from the Department of Motor Vehicles. Once I was summoned to appear before the TLC. I spent eight hours waiting for my case, and then I had to pay a fine of 150 dollars, a day's earnings.

Your only chance is to try and keep relaxed. If you let every negative thing that happens get at you, then your angst level shoots up and you have even more problems, you may even cause a crash. I've only had two small accidents that were my fault. Fender benders. Nothing else. There are taxi rentals who ditch you after three accidents. If you have a major crash, things get nasty anyway. If the police note down too many points, you're disqualified. I really don't know if I could carry on, or if I'd want to, after losing my license for a month.

It's not always easy to stay cool, though. Take the thing with the mugging, for example. It was early in the morning, and a man got in. He said he wanted to go to 164th Street. He didn't look particularly confidence-inspiring, certainly didn't look as if he had a lot of money, and 164th isn't a good address. Okay, halfway there he threatened me saying he had a piece (gun). We wrestled a bit. I didn't believe him. Not for too long though, he could have a knife. I gave him 20 dollars. Taxi driving in New York simply is and will continue to be a hard living. I've nothing against hard work, blue-collar jobs. I once worked as a chipper, throwing truck parts around and chipping off the flanges. Every day I carried a weight the equivalent of eight elephants, forty-five tons. That was honest work, and no one talked much. Just as art can be very honest, too.

My taxi is more than just a vehicle which I have to use to earn money. My taxi is my lens, my office, and gallery. Sometimes people order prints of my photos. Once while driving a party of four to another party location, one passenger asked what I made per hour. "I'll triple it, come shoot our party." They bought 12 prints.

Over several years, thousands of people have seen my pictures, countless have said they would definitely buy my book. Would I have had this backing, this publicity, any-where else? And some people just told me the taxi drive with me was the best they'd ever had in their life.

That's my real reward. It's not the money I earn with the cab. It's the human contact and what I see and photograph. When I don't earn any money, I at least have shot a roll or two. And I know that I'm digging for diamonds. Seen in this light, I haven't had a single bad day in my career as a New York cabbie.

Die Rastlosigkeit des Jägers
David Bradford über seinen Job als Cabbie

Manchmal fragt man sich, wie ein Schwarm Vögel scheinbar wirr durcheinander fliegen kann, ohne daß die Tiere zusammenstoßen. Wie? Weil sie sich in festgelegten Bahnen bewegen. So ist es auch mit Autos in New York. Wie können soviele von ihnen so hektisch und schnell durcheinanderfahren, ohne sich ineinander zu verkeilen? Auch jedes Auto hat eine unsichtbare Hoheitszone, die jeder respektiert. Taxifahren in New York ist nicht so gefährlich, wie es vielleicht auf den ersten Blick aussieht.

Dennoch: Wenn ich morgens ins Auto steige, fühle ich mich, als wäre ich für den Rest des Tages in einem Automobilrennen. Manche Taxifahrer tun alles, um eine Fuhre zu bekommen. Kreuzen die Fahrbahn. Biegen von der linken Spur nach rechts ab. Geschwindigkeitsüberschreitung, Fahrbahnwechsel, U-Turns, es wird alles praktiziert, was erlaubt und nicht erlaubt ist. Da draußen sind alle deine Konkurrenten, das ist nicht wie beim Football, wo du dem Mann mit derselben Trikotfarbe den Ball zuwirfst. Hier ist jedes gelbe Auto dein Konkurrent. Als New Yorker Taxifahrer hast du im Grunde keine Freunde auf der Straße. Der einzige Freund, den du hast, bist du selber.

Ich bin ein Jäger. Cabbies sind auf der Jagd. Du bist hungrig, wenn du keine Fuhre hast, und jede Fuhre ist ein kleiner Adrenalinstoß. Wenn du eine Weile niemanden aufgabeln kannst, wirst du unruhig. 35 Minuten ohne Fahrgast, Jeez! Du denkst daran, wieviel Geld du verdienen mußt. Was, schon wieder eine Stunde ohne Kundschaft? Mist! Dann ist man soweit, daß man an der Farbe seines Autos zweifelt. Ist es wirklich gelb? Dann passiert es. Direkt vor dir steht jemand, winkt und du bist eines von drei leeren Taxis an einer roten Ampel. Bäng – du hast im richtigen Moment aufgepaßt und die Fahrt gewonnen.

Man muß in diesem Geschäft geschickt sein, ein flüssiger Fahrer, sehr aufmerksam, psychisch stark. Du mußt die Straße vor dir im Blickfeld haben und die Situation im Rückspiegel, dein Verhalten ist vom Verhalten deiner Konkurrenten abhängig. Du mußt andere Taxis abhängen, du bleibst so lange in der mittleren Fahrspur, bis du eine Entscheidung treffen kannst. Es ist bei dichtem Verkehr immer eine kleine Existenzfrage, ob du dich auf der Straße links oder rechts hältst. Ich kenne den Schaltrhythmus jeder Ampel in der Stadt. Ich weiß, zu welcher Uhrzeit die Leute wo stehen.

120 Dollar Einnahmen nach Abzug der Unkosten sind das Maximum, Trinkgeld inklusive. Dann hatte man einen guten Tag. An einem wirklich schlechten Tag können es schon mal 30 Dollar sein. Im Schnitt macht ein guter New Yorker Cabbie 70 bis 80 Dollar täglich. Das sind im besten Fall 500 Dollar Wochenlohn für elf bis zwölf Stunden Arbeit an sechs Tagen in der Woche. Früher war die Situation für uns hier besser. Die Einnahmen wurden zwischen dem Vermieter des Wagens und dem Fahrer im Verhältnis 51 zu 49 Prozent gesplittet. Inzwischen nehmen die Garagen horrende Kommissionen dafür, daß sie dir ein Auto überlassen. 110, 120 Dollar pro Tag sind keine Seltenheit. Die Wochenrate kann 625 Dollar, manchmal sogar 650 Dollar betragen. Wer wegen des Geldes Taxi fahren muß, ist arm dran. Reich wird man jedenfalls nicht davon.

Dafür machst du jede Menge grotesker Erfahrungen. Neulich steigt ein Typ ein und gibt mir sieben Anweisungen, wie ich zu seinem Bestimmungsort zu fahren hätte. Ich sage: „Schon gut, die Hälfte davon kann ich mir immerhin merken." Manche Leute sind unerträglich, glauben, sie wären die Strecke öfter gefahren als jeder andere. Was glauben die, wie oft ich hier schon jede Strecke gefahren bin? Okay, der Typ wird pampig, fängt an, mit mir rumzudiskutieren und sagt beim Aussteigen: „Nebenbei bemerkt sind Sie auch noch ein ziemlich mediokrer Fotograf." Das war bösartig. Aber ich habe mir gedacht: „Warte nur, irgendwann werde ich mein Buch haben." Es passiert auch, daß man von allen und jedem einfach nur beschimpft wird, weil sie ihre schlechte Laune an einem auslassen wollen. Manche spucken Taxifahrer an, weil sie Taxifahrer eben nicht leiden können. Das sind Leute außerhalb des Taxis, über die ich spreche.

An manchen Tagen kommt alles zusammen. Du wirst aus der Fahrbahn bugsiert, jemand schnappt dir die Kundschaft weg, du entgehst knapp einem Unfall, es ist heiß, du steckst im Stau, weil in einer engen Straße ein Müllwagen rangiert, der im Zeitlupentempo die Abfallcontainer entleert. Wenn sich dann ein verschüchterter Autofahrer vor dir nicht traut, sich daran vorbeizuschlängeln, hängst du eine halbe Stunde lang fest. Das kann deinen Tag ruinieren. Du machst kaum Kohle, verlierst immens viel Zeit und bist moralisch angeschlagen. Dann kommt dir die Karre wie dein eigenes Gefängnis vor. Von Strafzetteln wollen wir gar nicht erst reden. Manchmal brummen sie dir wegen eines Vergehens gleich zwei Tickets auf. Einen kriegt man von der TLC, den anderen vom Department of Motor Vehicles. Einmal hatte ich eine Vorladung bei der TLC, acht Stunden habe ich auf meine Verhandlung gewartet, um dann 150 Dollar Strafe, einen Tagesverdienst, zu löhnen. Du hast nur eine Chance, du mußt versuchen, relaxed zu bleiben. Wenn du dich von jeder negativen Sache einnehmen läßt, dann geht dein Angstlevel in die Höhe, dann hast du noch mehr Probleme, baust womöglich sogar einen Crash. Ich hatte erst zwei kleine Unfälle, an denen ich schuld war. *Fender benders* – Stoßstangenverbieger. Sonst nichts. Es gibt Taxiverleihe, die werfen dich nach drei Unfällen raus. Wenn du einen größeren Crash hast, wird es ohnehin unangenehm. Wenn die Polizei zuviele Punkte notiert, hast du Fahrverbot. Ich wüßte echt nicht, ob ich noch weitermachen könnte und wollte, wenn ich einen Monat lang keine Lizenz hätte.

Es ist aber nicht leicht, immer cool zu bleiben. Da war zum Beispiel die Geschichte mit dem Überfall. Es war frühmorgens und ein Mann stieg ein. Er sagte, er wolle in die 164th Street. Der Mann sah nicht besonders vertrauensselig aus, jedenfalls nicht nach Geld, und 164th ist keine gute Adresse. Okay, auf halbem Weg bedrohte er mich und sagte, er hätte eine Kanone. Wir kämpften ein bißchen. Ich glaubte ihm nicht. Dennoch hätte er immerhin ein Messer haben können. Ich habe ihm 20 Dollar gegeben. Taxifahren in New York ist und bleibt einfach ein hartes Gewerbe. Ich habe nichts gegen harte Arbeit, Blaumannjobs. Ich habe mal als Zuschneider gearbeitet. Lastwagenteile herumgeworfen und den Flansch abgeschnitten. Da habe ich jeden Tag das Gewicht von acht Elefanten transportiert. 45 Tonnen. Das war eine ehrliche Arbeit, da wurde nicht viel rumgequatscht. So wie Kunst sehr ehrlich sein kann.

Mein Taxi ist mehr als nur ein Vehikel, mit dem ich Geld verdienen muß. Mein Taxi ist mein Objektiv, mein Büro und meine Galerie. Manchmal bestellen Leute Abzüge meiner Fotos. Einmal habe ich eine Gruppe von vier Leuten zu einer Party gefahren, als ein Fahrgast fragte, was ich in einer Stunde verdiene. „Ich verdreifache es. Komm mit und fotografiere unsere Party." Sie haben 12 Abzüge gekauft. Über die Jahre haben Tausende meine Bilder gesehen, viele haben gesagt, sie würden definitiv mein Buch kaufen. Hätte ich diese Bestätigung und Werbung woanders gehabt? Und manche sagen einfach nur, die Taxifahrt mit mir sei die beste ihres Lebens gewesen.

Das ist die wahre Belohnung für mich. Es geht nicht um das Geld, das ich mit dem Cab verdiene. Es geht um Kontakte mit Menschen, und es geht darum, was ich sehe, was ich fotografiere. Wenn ich kein Geld verdiene, bekomme ich wenigstens immer ein oder zwei belichtete Filme zustande. Und ich weiß, daß ich dabei nach Diamanten grabe. So gesehen hatte ich in meiner Karriere als New Yorker Cabbie keinen einzigen schlechten Tag.

Toujours à l'affût tel le chasseur
David Bradford au sujet de son boulot comme cabbie

Je me demande parfois comment une nuée d'oiseaux peut voler apparemment de façon désordonnée sans que les animaux ne se télescopent. Comment ? Eh bien, parce qu'ils se déplacent dans une direction bien précise. Il en est de même pour les voitures à New York. Comment autant de véhicules peuvent-ils circuler si nerveusement et si vite les uns entre les autres sans s'accrocher ? Chaque auto a une zone de souveraineté invisible que chacun respecte. Conduire un taxi à New York n'est pas aussi dangereux qu'il y paraît peut-être à première vue.

Et pourtant, quand je monte en voiture le matin, j'ai l'impression de prendre le départ d'une course automobile qui va durer le reste de la journée. Certains conducteurs de taxi ne reculent devant rien pour obtenir une course. Ils traversent la chaussée de part en part. Bifurquent à droite, depuis la file de gauche. Commettent un excès de vitesse, changent de voie sans prévenir, font demi-tour au carrefour ; ils font tout ce qui est autorisé et tout ce qui ne l'est pas. Là, dehors, chaque taxi est un concurrent, ce n'est pas comme au football où tu fais une passe à l'homme qui porte le même maillot que toi. Ici, chaque auto jaune est au fond ton ennemi. En tant que chauffeur de taxi new-yorkais, tu n'as aucun ami sur la route. Le seul ami que tu aies, c'est toi-même.

Je suis un chasseur. Les cabbies vont à la chasse. Tu es affamé lorsque tu n'as pas de trajet et chaque course est une petite montée d'adrénaline. Si tu restes un moment sans être hélé par quelqu'un, tu deviens nerveux. 35 minutes sans passager, bon Dieu ! Tu te mets alors à penser à l'argent que tu dois gagner. Quoi, encore une autre heure de passée sans un seul client ? Bordel ! C'est le moment où on commence alors à douter de la couleur de sa voiture. Est-elle vraiment jaune ? C'est alors qu'il se passe quelque chose. Il y a quelqu'un qui vous fait signe et vous vous retrouvez avec deux autres taxis vides au feu rouge. Bang : tu as vraiment été vigilant et tu décroches la course.

Dans ce métier, il faut être habile et avoir les nerfs solides. Tu ne dois pas perdre une miette de ce qui se passe sur la route devant toi sans jamais oublier de jeter un coup d'œil dans ton rétroviseur, ton comportement dépend de celui de tes concurrents. Tu dois semer les autres taxis, tu restes scotché sur la voie du milieu jusqu'à ce que tu puisses prendre une décision. Quand il y a beaucoup de circulation, savoir si tu vas rester sur la file de gauche ou passer sur celle de droite est un peu une question existentielle. Je connais le rythme de passage au rouge de chaque feu dans cette ville. Je sais exactement à quelle heure et dans quel coin ça bouchonne.

120 dollars après déduction des faux frais, c'est vraiment le maximum, pourboires compris. Alors, on peut dire qu'on a fait une bonne journée. Les jours de vaches maigres, on tourne plutôt autour des 30 dollars. En moyenne, un cabbie new-yorkais gagne entre 70 et 80 dollars par jour. Dans le meilleur des cas, cela représente un salaire hebdomadaire de 500 dollars pour 11 à 12 heures de travail à raison de six jours par semaine. Autrefois, les choses allaient mieux pour nous. Le loueur de la voiture percevait 51 % des recettes, le reste revenant au chauffeur. Maintenant, les garages prélèvent une commission astronomique pour te céder une voiture. Il n'est pas rare qu'on te demande 110 à 120 dollars par jour. Le taux hebdomadaire peut atteindre 625 dollars, parfois même 650. Celui qui doit conduire un taxi pour gagner de l'argent n'est vraiment pas dans une situation enviable. En tout cas, ce n'est pas avec ce boulot qu'on peut faire fortune.

En revanche, tu fais des quantités d'expériences grotesques. Tout récemment, un type est monté et m'a donné sept instructions sur la façon dont je devais le conduire à sa destination. Je lui dis : « C'est bon, je vais pouvoir me rappeler au moins la moitié. » Certains clients sont insupportables, ils pensent avoir déjà fait le trajet plus souvent que tous les autres. Mais savent-ils combien de fois j'ai parcouru ici chaque trajet ? Okay, le type devient hargneux, commence à me critiquer à propos de tout et de rien et lance en descendant : « Soit dit en passant, vous êtes en plus un photographe assez médiocre. » C'était d'une méchanceté gratuite. Mais je me suis dit : « Attends mon gars, un de ces jours, je l'aurai mon livre ». Il arrive aussi que l'on se fasse insulter sous un prétexte quelconque, par tous ceux qui ont envie de se défouler. Il y en a qui crachent sur les chauffeurs de taxi tout simplement parce qu'ils ne peuvent pas les souffrir. Ces gens dont je parle gravitent autour des conducteurs de taxi.

Certains jours, tout arrive en même temps. On t'éjecte brutalement de la voie de circulation, quelqu'un te pique un client sous le nez, tu passes à deux doigts d'un accident, il fait chaud, tu es coincé dans un embouteillage parce que des éboueurs se garent dans une ruelle étroite et vident leur benne pleine de détritus comme dans un film au ralenti. Si un automobiliste intimidé devant toi n'ose pas se faufiler à côté, tu peux rester coincé une demi-heure entre deux pâtés de maisons. Cela peut te ruiner ta journée. Tu ne fais pratiquement pas de pognon. Tu perds énormément de temps et ça te fiche le moral à zéro. Alors, ta bagnole te donne l'impression d'être ta propre prison. Et encore, je ne parle pas des contredanses. Parfois, ils t'en collent deux d'un seul coup pour une infraction. On s'en fait coller une par la TLC et l'autre, par le Department of Motor Vehicles. Une fois, j'ai été convoqué à la TLC, j'ai attendu huit heures avant de passer devant le juge pour finalement payer 150 dollars d'amende, parfois ce que je gagne en une journée.

Ton unique chance, c'est de rester cool. Si tu te prends la tête à cause du moindre pépin, la frousse t'envahit, tes ennuis commencent et il arrive même alors que tu aies une vraie collision. Je n'ai causé que deux accidents. *Fender benders*. Pare-chocs tordu. Sinon, rien. Il y a des loueurs de taxi qui te licencient au bout de trois accidents. Si tu as un crash plus sérieux, les choses deviennent franchement désagréables. Quand la police note trop de points, c'est le retrait de permis. Je ne sais vraiment pas si j'aurais encore l'envie et la volonté de continuer si on me privait de licence pendant un mois.

Mais ce n'est pas si facile de rester tout le temps cool. Il y a eu, par exemple, l'histoire du hold-up. C'était tôt le matin, un homme est monté dans mon taxi. Il m'a dit qu'il voulait se rendre à la 164ᵉ Rue. L'homme n'inspirait pas particulièrement confiance, il avait l'air fauché, et la 164ᵉ est mal famée. Okay, à mi-chemin, il m'a menacé en me disant qu'il avait un revolver sur lui. On s'est empoigné. Je ne le croyais pas. Mais je n'étais pas loin de penser qu'il pouvait avoir un couteau et je lui ai donné 20 dollars. Ensuite, il s'est tiré. Conduire un taxi à New York est et reste tout simplement un dur métier. Je n'ai rien contre l'idée de travailler dur, de porter un bleu de travail. J'ai, une fois, travaillé pour une firme de montage. A porter et à riveter des pièces de camion. J'ai alors transporté par jour le poids de huit éléphants. 45 tonnes ! C'était un travail honnête, on ne gaspillait pas son temps en parlotes. Tout comme l'art peut être très honnête.

Mon taxi est plus qu'un simple véhicule avec lequel je dois gagner de l'argent. Mon taxi est mon objectif, mon bureau et ma galerie. Parfois, des gens commandent des tirages de mes photos. Une fois, en pleine nuit, alors que je conduisais quatre passagers à une soirée, l'un d'eux m'a demandé ce que je gagnais par heure. Il m'a proposé le triple si je prenais quelques photos lors de sa soirée. Ils m'ont acheté 12 tirages. Des milliers de visiteurs ont pu voir mes photos, beaucoup ont dit qu'ils achèteraient un de mes livres. Aurais-je eu cette confirmation et cette publicité ailleurs ? Et certains ont dit tout simplement et sans ambages que c'est avec moi qu'ils ont fait le meilleur trajet en taxi de toute leur vie.

C'est ça la véritable récompense pour moi. Et non pas l'argent que je gagne avec le cab. Ce qui m'intéresse, c'est le contact avec les gens, c'est ce que je vois, ce que je photographie. Si je ne gagne pas d'argent, je m'en tire au moins toujours avec un film ou deux. Je sais que je vais trouver des diamants. Vu sous cet angle, de toute ma carrière de cabbie new-yorkais, je n'ai pas eu une seule mauvaise journée.

Domingo and Dominas
David Bradford on Encounters in the Taxi and in Real Life

Driving a taxi is a privilege. It is also one of the best methods of studying people. What they say. How they think. Why they behave as they do behave or why they dress as they do dress. Each has his own tale to tell. Sometimes I'd like to have a tape-recorder on hand and record their conversations, documenting everything along with the noise of the street and the sounds of the car.

You meet the most incredible people. And I don't mean all the celebrities. It's impossible to work as a taxi driver in New York without meeting some star or other. I've had a great conversation with Robert Duvall and actress Lauren Hutton. The director Woody Allen and his wife crossed at a zebra crossing just in front of me. Even Bill Clinton (then candidate) walked by my cab. The composer Philip Glass was a passenger, and we talked about cab driving experiences, he drove a cab for three years. I've given a lift to Placido Domingo and complimented him on his voice, and he responded in kind by complimenting me on my pictures. But so-called "ordinary" people are more generous with their tips than celebrities. Perhaps they are better able to put a value on a tough job.

The biggest surprises, in any case, you get with people who seem to look normal. Once a woman stood in the street waving so hesitantly that I thought she was shy. As it turned out, she worked as a dominatrix. Another time, a girl got in and told me how she worked for a mortician. I asked, "How do you come to work in a place like that?" I like talking to the clientele. You discover the craziest things. As it happened, the girl worked in the family business. She said, the thing she always found worst was having to prepare the bodies of people who had died at her age. She was maybe in her early twenties. She went on to tell me which parts of a corpse were the most difficult to embalm. Within a few minutes, I've had a TV host, a nurse, a transvestite and an exhibitionist who undressed down to her underwear. Crazy.

Others are drunk, on ecstasy, or simply fall asleep, and then I don't know whereabouts in Brooklyn I should drop them off. One Saturday before six in the morning a young man escaped into my taxi after he'd been dreadfully beaten up by two other guys. I didn't ask and he didn't say. I just provided escape. When I pick up young mothers with their newborn babies outside a hospital, the trip's always free. Once I picked the same woman up twice in one week. Must be fate and we began to date. But somehow nothing came of it. The affair didn't last long.

I live alone. You remember the trombonist from the New York Philharmonic? We talked about music. I once played the trombone myself. Anyway, the guy said I had a soloistic talent. He was right, I'm not someone who seeks company. What I do is art, and while doing it, I'm on my own. I appreciate revelations, there is nothing quite like them and these seem to happen more often within my own experience.

Von Domingo und Dominas
David Bradford über Begegnungen im Taxi und im richtigen Leben

Ein Taxi zu fahren ist ein Privileg. Es ist ebenfalls eine der besten Methoden, Menschen zu studieren. Was sie reden. Wie sie denken. Warum sie sich so benehmen, wie sie sich benehmen, oder wieso sie sich so kleiden, wie sie sich kleiden. Jeder hat seine Geschichte. Manchmal würde ich gerne ein Tonbandgerät dabeihaben und ihre Unterhaltungen aufzeichnen, alles dokumentieren, zusammen mit dem Straßenlärm und den Geräuschen des Wagens.

Man trifft hier auf die unglaublichsten Leute. Damit meine ich gar nicht all die Prominenten. Es ist unmöglich, in New York als Taxifahrer zu arbeiten und keinem Star zu begegnen. Ich hatte eine großartige Unterhaltung mit Robert Duvall und der Schauspielerin Lauren Hutton. Der Regisseur Woody Allen und seine junge Frau liefen vor mir über den Zebrastreifen. Sogar Bill Clinton (zu der Zeit noch Kandidat) lief einmal neben meinem Taxi her. Der Komponist Philip Glass fuhr mit mir, und wir tauschten Taxifahrer-Erfahrungen aus, weil er selber drei Jahre lang Taxi gefahren ist. Ich habe Placido Domingo befördert und ihm ein Kompliment gemacht für seine Stimme, wofür er sich mit einem Kompliment für meine Bilder revanchierte. Beim Trinkgeld sind aber die sogenannten 'einfachen' Leute großzügiger als Celebrities. Vielleicht wissen sie es mehr zu schätzen, was es bedeutet, einen harten Job zu haben.

Die größten Überraschungen erlebt man sowieso mit Leuten, die vermeintlich normal aussehen. Einmal stand eine Frau an der Straße und winkte so zaghaft, daß ich dachte, sie sei schüchtern. Wie sich herausstellte, arbeitete sie als Domina. Ein anderes Mal stieg ein Mädchen ein und erzählte, sie arbeite in einem Bestattungsunternehmen. Ich fragte: „Wie kommen Sie denn zu so einem Job?" Ich unterhalte mich manchmal gerne mit der Kundschaft. Man erfährt dabei die irrsten Dinge. Na ja, das Mädchen arbeitete in einem Familienunternehmen. Sie sagte, am schlimmsten seien immer die Fälle, in denen sie Tote präparieren müsse, die in ihrem Alter gestorben seien. Sie war vielleicht Anfang 20. Sie erzählte mir dann noch, welche Körperpartien einer Leiche besonders schwierig zu mumifizieren sind. Man hat innerhalb weniger Minuten einen Moderator vom Fernsehen, eine Krankenschwester, einen Transvestiten und eine Exhibitionistin im Auto, die sich freimacht bis auf die Unterwäsche. Verrückt.

Andere sind betrunken, auf Ecstasy oder pennen einfach nur ein, und ich weiß dann nicht, wo ich sie in Brooklyn abladen soll. An einem Samstag vor sechs Uhr morgens hat sich ein junger Mann in mein fahrendes Taxi geflüchtet, nachdem er vorher von zwei Männern schrecklich verprügelt worden war. Ich habe ihn nicht gefragt, was passiert war und er sagte auch nichts. Ich stellte ihm einfach eine Fluchtmöglichkeit zur Verfügung. Wenn ich junge Mütter mit ihren Neugeborenen vor einem Krankenhaus einsammle, ist der Trip immer umsonst. Einmal fuhr eine Frau in derselben Woche zweimal mit mir. Wir sagten uns, das muß Schicksal sein und haben angefangen, miteinander auszugehen. Aber irgendwie ist daraus nichts geworden, unsere Affäre hat nicht lange gehalten.

Ich lebe allein. Sie erinnern sich an den Posaunisten von den New Yorker Philharmonikern? Wir sprachen über Musik. Ich habe selber mal Posaune gespielt. Der Typ sagte jedenfalls, ich hätte ein solistisches Talent. Der Mann hatte recht, ich bin kein Mensch, der Gesellschaft sucht. Was ich mache, ist Kunst, und dabei bin ich auf mich selbst gestellt. Ich schätze Offenbarungen; es gibt nichts Vergleichbares. Sie scheinen jedoch häufiger innerhalb meiner eigenen Erfahrung vorzukommen.

Rencontres avec Domingo et domina
David Bradford au sujet de ses rencontres en taxi et dans la vie de tous les jours

Conduire un taxi est un privilège. C'est l'une des meilleures méthodes pour étudier les hommes. Ce qu'ils disent. Ce qu'ils pensent. Leur comportement, leur façon de s'habiller. Chacun a son histoire. Parfois, j'aimerais bien avoir un magnétophone avec moi et enregistrer ce qu'ils me racontent, tout documenter conjointement avec les rumeurs de la circulation et les bruits de la voiture.

On rencontre ici les gens les plus incroyables. Et encore, je ne fais même pas allusion à toutes les célébrités. Il est impossible de travailler comme chauffeur de taxi à New York sans rencontrer de stars. J'ai eu de super discussions avec l'acteur David Duvall, l'actrice Lauren Hutton. Le metteur en scène Woody Allen et sa jeune épouse ont franchi devant moi un passage clouté. J'ai même vu un jour Bill Clinton, alors candidat, marcher dans la rue, près de mon taxi. Le compositeur Philip Glass a circulé à bord de mon taxi et nous avons parlé des cabbies, parce qu'il avait lui-même été chauffeur de taxi pendant trois ans. J'ai transporté Placido Domingo et je l'ai félicité pour sa voix, et lui m'a renvoyé l'ascenseur en me faisant un compliment sur mes photos. Mais, pour ce qui est des pourboires, les gens que l'on dit « simples » sont plus généreux que les celebrities. Sans doute savent-ils mieux ce que cela signifie d'avoir un boulot difficile.

Les plus grandes surprises, on les a, de toute façon, avec les gens que l'on qualifierait de « normaux ». Un jour, une femme attendait au bord de la rue et hélait les taxis avec tant d'hésitation que je l'ai crue timide. En réalité, il s'est avéré qu'elle travaillait comme domina. Une autre fois, une fille est montée et m'a raconté qu'elle travaillait dans une entreprise de pompes funèbres. Je lui ai demandé : « Comment pouvez-vous faire un tel métier ? » Parfois, j'aime bien discuter avec la clientèle. On apprend à cette occasion les choses les plus loufoques. En fait, la jeune fille travaillait tout simplement dans une entreprise familiale. Elle me dit que, le pire, c'était d'embaumer des morts qui avaient le même âge qu'elle. Elle avait peut-être une vingtaine d'années. Elle m'a raconté alors quelles parties du corps étaient les plus difficiles à momifier. En l'espace de quelques minutes, on se retrouve en compagnie d'un présentateur télé, d'une infirmière, d'un travelo et d'une exhibitionniste qui se déshabille jusqu'aux sous-vêtements. Dingue.

D'autres sont ivres morts, ont pris de l'ecstasy ou s'endorment sur la banquette et je ne sais pas où je dois les déposer dans Brooklyn. Un samedi à six heures du matin, un jeune homme s'est réfugié dans mon taxi après avoir été auparavant effroyablement molesté par deux autres types. Je ne lui ai pas parlé et je ne lui ai rien demandé. Il n'a rien dit lui non plus. Je lui ai juste offert un refuge ; il était vraiment dans un piteux état. Quand je passe chercher de jeunes mères avec leur nouveau-né devant un hôpital, la course est toujours gratuite. Une fois, la même femme a fait à deux reprises un trajet avec moi en une seule semaine. C'était sans aucun doute un signe du destin et nous avons commencé à sortir ensemble. Mais, ça n'a rien donné. Notre liaison n'a pas duré bien longtemps.

Je vis seul. Vous vous rappelez le joueur de trombone de l'Orchestre philharmonique de New York ? Nous avons parlé musique. J'ai moi-même joué autrefois du trombone. En tout cas, le type disait que j'avais un talent de soliste. L'homme avait raison. Je ne suis pas le genre de type qui recherche la société. Ce que je fais, c'est de l'art et, pour ça, j'aime être seul. J'aime les révélations, c'est ce que j'aime le plus et elles se produisent souvent lorsque je suis seul.

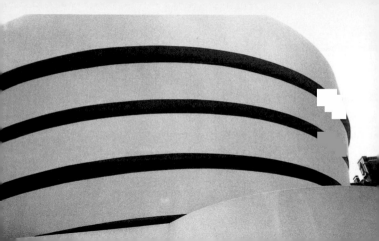

First Manhattan, then Berlin
David Bradford on Art, Photography and Future Plans

I remember it well. It was in 1996. I'd had three commissions from the *New Yorker* to photograph Manhattan. The theater district by day and Times Square and West Village at night. All from the taxi of course. The people at the magazine loved the shots, but for some reason or other, it didn't lead to another assignment. Maybe the disappointment showed on my face, but as I was going down in the elevator with the photo editor she said, "Don't worry, David, one day you'll be famous." It would have been a small dream come true to draw for the *New Yorker*. This had been in my imagination for years. I did have some close calls with them. I had always enjoyed drawing city buildings, the older the better. You can find more character in these structures than you do in many people. I believe that all the time I have put into drawing has paved the way for me to photograph in the manner I do. I studied dance and gymnastics as well. I think these disciplines taught me a sense of space and movement. Who would have thought that people would be interested in what comes out of a little black box that I hold in my hand while driving?

I like the drawings of Klimt, Matisse, Cocteau and Schiele. The single line can be so revealing. Cocteau considered drawing to be handwriting which was untied and then retied in a different fashion. All these painters really penetrated through to people's souls, their lives. It all depends on how one looks at the world, how you see through your eyes, not just with them.

Photography has interested me for as long as I can remember. I've always looked at
the works of the great masters, bought myself books. On 18th Street near Fifth Avenue
there's a bookstore with old photography books galore. I could spend a whole day
there. After one of my landlords had compensated me for a change of apartment,
I bought myself a Leica M6. That was an investment of 4,000 dollars. An enormous
amount of money by my standards, but every shot I took bowled me over.
Atget, Kertész, Evans, Lartigue – these are people I can relate to. I like spontaneous
photography, not a posed situation. All the technology in the world won't help you
if you don't have the ability to recognize great pictures. Shortly before his death I
met Alfred Eisenstaedt. He was introduced to me while I was visiting the offices of
LIFE magazine. After the article about me I had been invited to pay a visit. Eisenstaedt
shook me by the hand and said I had a good eye. To have your work complimented
by such a master is unusual. As for all the other talk about my pictures, I sometimes
think they're talking about someone else.

I once had Richard Avedon in the taxi, and he asked me who my favorite photographer
was. So I said Kertész. Avedon said, "But he's dead." I said, "And so's Bach." Avedon
asked about a living photographer. I said, "Maybe Salgado." He made no further
comment. Maybe he was disappointed I hadn't recognized him. Really, I didn't
know who I was driving around. When he said he took photographs too, I asked in
all innocence, "What do you photograph then?" "Portraits", he said, "and a bit of
fashion." Then he told me his name. "What an encounter," I thought to myself.
But what was I supposed to say at that moment?

When is something beautiful in my eyes? When everything works together, when a
composition is born. When one sentence leads on to the next, when one thought
creates a new thought. When one is not just visually stimulated, or acoustically, but
mentally too. Beauty means that more depth is present than one sees at first sight. It is
harmony. Harmony creates beauty. Beauty is perfect. Take the music of Bach. It is so
beautiful and perfect, that sometimes you wonder was that sad or happy? Maybe both.

A Japanese film director once made a wonderful short film about me. He thanked me
by writing a little letter which said, "You overcome the reality of this world, which is
actually lousy, and photograph it so that it becomes art." Maybe my pictures are indeed
beautiful. But I can't say that. Vis-à-vis myself, I'm highly critical. It rarely happens that
I'm totally satisfied with one of my shots.

Nor can I say whether my photography has improved over the years. When I started,
I certainly didn't realize exactly what things are possible with pictures. That's changed.
Now I have some idea. I take care not to repeat myself in my work. I now more
intensively seek motifs which stand out. I no longer want to work so much with

the steering wheel as a stylistic device. I no longer want to take too many pictures in which there are no people. I no longer want to concentrate just on buildings, trees or the interior of the taxi. I'm looking for more balance. That's difficult. People are moving the whole time. You have to anticipate their movements. Every artist must continually try to experiment, to find a new approach.

I would like to photograph many cities in the world from a taxi. I like the element of chance to which one is subject in a taxi. Not to know what one's going to do, not knowing where you'll go next. No: people tell me where to go. They enter my life and dictate the way to me. It is what I do along the way with my own vision that counts. I think I shall always feel the desire to drive a taxi. It is such an intense experience and memory that I'm sure I can never forget it. Besides, I've been doing it for quite a long time. I once read in a book by a former convict who'd been in jail for 30 years. After his release he no longer knew how to unlock a door. That's funny. Didn't I say the taxi was my prison? Who knows what the consequences of my long-term incarceration will be.

There's a song by Leonard Cohen. It goes, "First we take Manhattan, then we take Berlin." Berlin would be exciting. New York and Berlin have something in common. After the opening of eastern Europe, Berlin could become the New York City of Europe. I also feel strongly attracted toward German culture. When the German television people from the ARD saw my pictures, they said the photos reminded them of German avant-garde photography. I think Berlin will be my next project. I could imagine visiting a total of ten capitals: Tokyo, Budapest, Paris, London... There are so many places that fascinate me. I try to remain open. My motto is "Be prepared!" You have to be able to react to life. I have played trombone, studied dance and done choreography. I have done gymnastics and worked as a draughtsman and a photographic assistant. All this has made me better. I have learned from everything. I have tried my whole life simply to absorb as much as possible.

And if life should come round the next corner and say, "Hello, David Bradford!" I would answer, "Hey, let's go." Then we'll have another marriage, life and me.

Zuerst Manhattan, dann Berlin
David Bradford über Kunst, Fotografie und Zukunftspläne

Ich erinnere mich noch ganz genau. Es war 1996. Ich hatte vom *New Yorker* drei Aufträge bekommen, Manhattan zu fotografieren. Theater District bei Tag und Times Square sowie West Village bei Nacht. Natürlich alles vom Taxi aus. Die Leute von der Zeitung mochten die Aufnahmen, doch aus irgendeinem Grund kam es nicht zu neuen Aufträgen. Vielleicht war die Enttäuschung in mein Gesicht geschrieben, aber als ich mit der Fotoredakteurin im Aufzug nach unten fuhr, sagte sie zu mir: „Mach' Dir keine Sorgen, David, Du wirst einmal berühmt sein."

Es wäre für mich die Erfüllung eines kleinen Traumes gewesen, für das *New Yorker* zu zeichnen. Diese Vorstellung hatte ich schon seit Jahren. Tatsächlich hatte ich auch einige vielversprechende Telefonate mit ihnen. Ich hatte immer ein Faible für alte Gebäude – je älter desto besser. Die Strukturen dieser Gebäude sind ausdrucksstärker als manche Menschen. Ich glaube, daß all die Zeit, die ich in die Zeichnerei gesteckt habe, mir den Weg zur Fotografie, so wie ich sie heute betreibe, geebnet hat. Ich habe auch Tanz und Gymnastik studiert. Diese Disziplinen haben mich gelehrt, einen Sinn für Raum und Bewegung zu entwickeln. Wer hätte gedacht, daß die Leute sich nun dafür interessieren, was aus einen kleinen schwarzen Kasten kommt, den ich beim Fahren in der Hand halte?

Ich mag die Zeichnungen von Klimt, Matisse, Cocteau und Schiele. Eine einzige Linie kann so viel aufdecken. Cocteau betrachtete das Zeichnen als eine Handschrift, die aufgelöst wird und dann wieder in einer anderen Form zusammenfließt. All diese Maler drangen wirklich zur Seele der Menschen, zu deren Leben vor. Es kommt darauf an, wie man auf die Welt schaut; es kommt nicht darauf an, was man sieht, sondern wie man es sieht.

Fotografie hat mich von jeher interessiert. Ich habe mir immer die Arbeiten der großen Meister angesehen, habe mir Bücher besorgt. In der 18th Street nahe der Fifth Avenue gibt es einen Buchladen mit einer Fülle von alten Bänden über Fotografie. Da könnte ich einen ganzen Tag lang rumstöbern. Nachdem ich von einem Vermieter für einen Wohnungswechsel eine Abfindung erhalten hatte, kaufte ich mir eine Leica M6. Das war eine Investition von 4000 Dollar. Unheimlich viel Geld für meine Verhältnisse, aber jede Aufnahme hat mich umgehauen. Atget, Kertész, Evans, Lartigue – das sind Leute, zu denen ich eine Verbindung spüre. Ich mag spontane Fotografie, nicht eine inszenierte Situation. Alle Technik der Welt hilft dir nichts, wenn du nicht die Fähigkeit hast, große Bilder zu erkennen. Kurz vor seinem Tod habe ich Alfred Eisenstaedt kennengelernt. Er wurde mir vorgestellt, als ich die Redaktion des *LIFE*-Magazins besuchte. Man hatte mich nach dem Artikel über mich zu einem Besuch eingeladen. Eisenstaedt hat mir die Hand geschüttelt und gesagt, ich hätte ein gutes Auge. Es ist ein ungewöhnlicher Moment, wenn deine Arbeit von so einem großen Meister gelobt wird. Bei all dem anderen Gerede über meine Bilder denke ich manchmal, die reden über einen anderen.

Als ich damals Richard Avedon im Taxi hatte, hat der mich gefragt, wer mein Lieblingsfotograf sei. Also sagte ich Kertész. Avedon meinte: „Aber der ist doch tot." Ich sagte: „Das ist Bach auch." Avedon fragte nach einem lebenden Fotografen. Ich sagte: „Vielleicht Salgado." Das hat er dann nicht mehr kommentiert. Vielleicht war er enttäuscht, daß ich ihn nicht erkannt habe. Wirklich, ich wußte nicht, wen ich da spazierenfahre. Als er sagte, er fotografiere auch, fragte ich noch ganz unschuldig: „Was fotografieren Sie denn so?" Er sagte „Portraits und ein bißchen Mode" und dann seinen Namen. „Was für eine Begegnung", dachte ich mir. Aber was sollte ich in diesem Moment noch sagen?

Wann etwas aus meiner Sicht schön ist? Wenn alles zusammenarbeitet, eine Komposition entsteht. Wenn ein Satz zum nächsten Satz führt, ein Gedanke einen neuen Gedanken kreiert. Wenn man nicht nur optisch oder akustisch animiert wird, sondern auch geistig. Schönheit bedeutet, daß mehr Tiefe vorhanden ist, als man auf den ersten Blick sieht. Es ist Harmonie. Harmonie kreiert Schönheit. Schönheit ist vollkommen. Nehmen Sie nur mal die Musik von Bach. Die ist so schön und vollkommen, daß man sich manchmal fragt: War der eigentlich traurig oder glücklich? Vielleicht beides.

Ein japanischer Filmregisseur hat mal einen wunderbaren Kurzfilm über mich gedreht. Der Mann hat mir zum Dank einen kleinen Brief geschrieben. In dem stand: „Du überwindest die Realität dieser Welt, die eigentlich beschissen ist, und fotografierst sie so, daß sie zu Kunst wird." Vielleicht sind meine Bilder tatsächlich schön. Aber das kann ich nicht sagen, ich bin mir gegenüber sehr kritisch, es kommt selten vor, daß ich mit einem meiner Bilder völlig zufrieden bin.

Ich kann auch nicht sagen, ob meine Fotografie über die Jahre besser geworden ist. Als ich anfing, habe ich sicherlich nicht genau gewußt, was mit Bildern möglich ist. Das hat sich verändert. Mittlerweile weiß ich besser Bescheid. Und ich bin bemüht, daß ich mich in meiner Arbeit nicht wiederhole. Ich suche nun intensiver nach Motiven, die sich abheben, die herausstechen. Ich will nicht mehr so viel mit dem Lenkrad als Stilmittel arbeiten. Ich will nicht mehr zu viele Bilder machen, auf denen keine Menschen vorkommen. Ich will mich nicht mehr nur auf Architektur, Bäume oder den Innenraum des Taxis konzentrieren. Ich suche nach mehr Ausgewogenheit. Das ist schwierig. Menschen bewegen sich ständig. Du mußt ihre Bewegungen vorausahnen. Jeder Künstler muß ständig experimentieren, versuchen, einen neuen Zugang zu finden.

Ich würde gerne viele große Städte der Welt aus dem Taxi fotografieren. Ich mag den Faktor Zufall, dem man im Taxi ausgesetzt ist. Nicht zu wissen, was man tun wird, wohin man als nächstes gehen wird. Nein, die Leute sagen mir, wohin ich zu gehen habe. Sie treten in mein Leben und diktieren mir den Weg. Es kommt darauf an, was ich mit meiner eigenen Sehweise entlang des Weges mache. Ich glaube, ich werde immer das Verlangen verspüren, Taxi zu fahren. Es ist eine so intensive Erfahrung und Erinnerung, daß ich sie wohl niemals vergessen kann. Außerdem mache ich es schon ziemlich lange. Ich habe in einem Buch über einen ehemaligen Häftling gelesen, der 30 Jahre im Gefängnis war. Nach seiner Entlassung wußte er nicht mehr, wie man eine Tür aufsperrt. Das ist lustig. Habe ich nicht gesagt, das Taxi ist mein Gefängnis? Wer weiß, welche Folgen meine langjährige Inhaftierung haben wird.

Es gibt ein Lied von Leonard Cohen. Darin heißt es: „First we take Manhattan, then we take Berlin." Berlin wäre spannend. New York und Berlin haben etwas Verbindendes. Berlin könnte nach der Öffnung Osteuropas das New York City von Europa werden. Ich fühle mich auch sehr stark zu deutscher Kultur hingezogen. Als die deutschen Fernsehleute von der ARD meine Bilder sahen, sagten sie, die Aufnahmen erinnerten sie an deutsche Avantgarde-Fotografie. Ich glaube, Berlin wird mein nächstes Projekt werden. Ich könnte mir vorstellen, insgesamt zehn Metropolen zu besuchen: Tokio, Budapest, Paris, London... Es gibt so viele Plätze, die mich faszinieren.

Ich versuche, offen zu bleiben. Mein Lebensmotto ist: „Sei vorbereitet!" Man muß in der Lage sein, auf das Leben zu reagieren. Ich habe Posaune gespielt und Tanz studiert, ich habe mich mit Choreographie beschäftigt und Gymnastik gemacht, ich habe als Zeichner und für Fotografen gearbeitet. Alles hat mich geprägt, von allem habe ich gelernt. Ich habe mein Leben lang so viel wie möglich absorbiert. Und wenn das Leben jetzt um die Ecke kommen sollte und sagen: „Hallo, David Bradford", dann antworte ich: „Hey, es geht los." Dann haben wir wieder eine Ehegemeinschaft, das Leben und ich.

D'abord Manhattan, ensuite Berlin
David Bradford au sujet de l'art, de la photographie et de ses projets d'avenir

Je m'en souviens bien. C'était en 1996. J'avais reçu trois commandes du *New Yorker*, je devais photographier Manhattan. Theater District le jour et la nuit, Times Square et West Village. Et cela, depuis le taxi, bien sûr. Les gens du magazine ont aimé les prises de vue. Mais, pour une raison que j'ignore, je n'ai pas reçu d'autre commande. La déception se lisait sur mon visage. Mais, un jour où je descendais en ascenseur avec la rédactrice photo, elle me dit : « Ne t'inquiète pas, David, un jour, tu seras célèbre. »

Naturellement, j'ai toujours eu pour objectif de faire une carrière d'artiste. Un rêve serait devenu réalité si j'avais réussi à travailler comme dessinateur pour le *New Yorker*. J'y ai pensé pendant des années. Nous nous sommes parlé plusieurs fois au téléphone. J'ai toujours aimé les vieux bâtiments de New York. J'ai un faible pour les vieilles pierres. Elles ont plus de caractère que certains êtres humains. Je pense que mes dessins ont constitué une étape décisive dans ma carrière de photographe. J'ai pris également des cours de danse et de gymnastique. Ces disciplines ont exacerbé mon sens de l'espace et du mouvement. Qui aurait cru que les gens allaient maintenant parler de moi parce que je fais des photos avec une petite boîte que je tiens dans mes mains tout en étant au volant de mon taxi ?

J'aime les dessins de Klimt, Matisse, Cocteau et Schiele. Un simple trait peut être tellement éloquent. Cocteau considérait le dessin comme une écriture qui se dénoue et épouse constamment une forme différente. Tous ces peintres pénètrent jusqu'à l'âme de l'homme, jusqu'à sa vie. Ce qui est important, c'est le regard que l'on porte sur le monde, la manière dont on le perçoit.

La photographie, aussi, m'a toujours intéressé. J'ai toujours regardé les travaux des grands maîtres, je me suis procuré des livres. Dans la 18e Rue près de la Cinquième Avenue, il y a une librairie qui est une véritable mine d'ouvrages photographiques. Je pourrais y passer des jours entiers. Avec les indemnités reçues un jour d'un propriétaire pour un changement d'appartement, je me suis acheté un Leica M6. C'était un investissement de 4 000 dollars. Une somme absolument faramineuse dans ma situation, mais chaque prise de vue m'a renversé. Atget, Kertész, Evans, Lartigue – ce sont là des gens dont je peux m'inspirer. J'aime la photographie spontanée, pas ces trucs mis en scène. Toute la technique du monde ne t'est d'aucun secours si tu n'es pas capable de reconnaître les grandes photos. Peu avant sa mort, j'ai fait la connaissance d'Alfred Eisenstaedt. Il m'a été présenté alors qu'il rendait visite à la rédaction du magazine *LIFE*. Après l'article qui m'avait été consacré, on m'avait envoyé une invitation. Eisenstaedt m'a serré la main et m'a dit que j'avais un œil exercé. C'est inhabituel que l'un des plus grands photographes de tous les temps te fasse des éloges sur ton travail. Lorsque j'entends les commentaires que l'on peut faire au sujet de mes photos, je pense parfois que les gens parlent de quelqu'un d'autre.

Le jour où j'avais Richard Avedon dans mon taxi, il m'a demandé qui était mon photographe préféré. Je lui ai répondu Kertész. Avedon a rétorqué : « Mais il est mort depuis longtemps. » Je lui ai répondu : « Bach aussi. » Avedon m'a dit « un photographe vivant ! » Je lui ai répondu : « Peut-être Salgado. » Alors, il n'a plus fait aucun commentaire. Peut-être était-il déçu que je ne l'aie pas reconnu. Vraiment, je ne savais pas qui était assis sur ma banquette arrière. Lorsqu'il m'a déclaré que lui aussi faisait de la photo, je lui ai encore demandé, tout à fait innocemment : « Et vous, vous photographiez quoi ? » Il m'a dit : « Des portraits et aussi un peu de mode » et il m'a dit son nom. « Quelle rencontre, ai-je pensé. Mais que dire de plus dans un tel moment ? »

Quand est-ce qu'une chose est belle selon moi ? Quand tout est cohérent, que cela donne naissance à une composition. Une phrase en entraîne une autre, une idée est à l'origine d'une nouvelle idée. Quand on n'est pas seulement inspiré sur le plan visuel, ou acoustique, mais aussi intellectuellement. Beauté signifie qu'il y a plus de pro-fondeur qu'on ne le remarque au premier coup d'œil. C'est l'harmonie. L'harmonie crée la beauté. La beauté est parfaite. Prenez par exemple la musique de Bach. Elle est si belle et si parfaite que l'on s'interroge parfois : était-il, en fait, triste, ou heureux ? Peut-être les deux à la fois.

Un metteur en scène japonais a, un jour, tourné un merveilleux court-métrage sur moi. Pour me remercier, l'homme m'a écrit une petite lettre. Dans celle-ci, il disait : « Tu surmontes la réalité de ce monde, qui est, à proprement parler, merdique, et tu la pho-tographies de telle manière qu'elle en devient un art. » Peut-être mes photos sont-elles réellement belles. Mais je ne peux guère en juger, je suis très critique à l'égard de mon travail, il est rare que je sois complètement satisfait de l'une de mes photos.

Je ne peux pas dire non plus si mes photos se sont améliorées au fil des ans. Lorsque j'ai commencé, je ne savais pas quelles possibilités offrait la photographie. Mais les choses ont changé. Désormais, j'arrive à m'en faire une idée. Et je m'efforce de ne pas me répéter dans mon travail. Je recherche désormais avec plus d'intensité des motifs qui se distinguent, se mettent en valeur. Je ne veux plus utiliser autant le volant comme moyen de style. Je veux faire davantage de photos sur lesquelles on voit des êtres humains. Je ne veux plus me concentrer seulement sur l'architecture, les arbres ou l'intérieur du taxi. Je recherche un peu plus d'équilibre. Mais c'est difficile. Les gens se déplacent en permanence. Tu dois anticiper leurs mouvements. Les bâtiments, par contre, ne se déplacent pas. Chaque artiste doit en permanence chercher à expérimenter, à trouver une nouvelle approche.

J'aimerais bien photographier de nombreuses villes du monde depuis un taxi. J'aime le facteur hasard auquel on est exposé dans un taxi. Ne pas savoir ce que l'on va faire, ne pas savoir quelle est sa prochaine destination. Non, les gens me disent où aller. Ils entrent dans ma vie et me dictent la voie à suivre. C'est ce qui se produit tout au long du trajet mais ma propre vision des choses est prédominante. Je crois que je ressentirai toujours le besoin de conduire un taxi. C'est une expérience si intense et un tel sou-venir qu'ils sont gravés à jamais dans ma mémoire. En outre, il y a déjà assez longtemps que je fais ça. J'ai lu dans un livre une histoire au sujet d'un ancien détenu qui avait passé trente ans en prison. Une fois libéré, il ne savait plus comment ouvrir une porte. C'est marrant. N'ai-je pas dit que le taxi était ma prison à moi ? Qui sait quelles conséquences vont avoir mes longues années de détention.

Il y a une chanson de Leonard Cohen qui dit : « First we take Manhattan, then we take Berlin. » Berlin serait une expérience passionnante. New York et Berlin ont quelque chose en commun. Depuis l'ouverture de l'Europe de l'Est, Berlin pourrait être la New York City d'Europe. Je me sens, d'ailleurs, très fortement attiré par la culture allemande.

Lorsque les cameramen de l'ARD, la chaîne de télévision allemande, ont vu mes photos, ils ont dit qu'elles leur rappelaient la photographie d'avant-garde allemande. Je pense que Berlin sera mon prochain projet. Je pourrais m'imaginer visiter au total dix métropoles : Tokyo, Budapest, Paris, Londres,... Il y a tant d'endroits qui me fascinent. J'essaie de conserver une ouverture d'esprit. Ma devise est : il faut être préparé, être en mesure de réagir à la vie. J'ai joué du trombone et fait des études de danse, j'ai pratiqué la chorégraphie et fait de la gymnastique. J'ai travaillé comme dessinateur et pour des photographes. Toutes les choses que j'ai apprises ont laissé en moi une empreinte indélébile. J'ai, tout simplement, durant ma vie entière, absorbé le plus de choses possible. Et, si la vie devait maintenant surgir brusquement au coin d'une rue et me dire : « Salut, David Bradford », je répondrais : « Et, on y va ! » Alors nous aurions de nouveau une vie conjugale, la vie et moi.

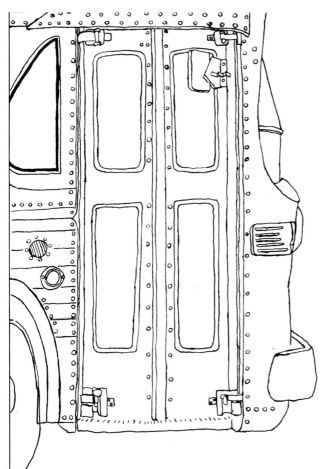

A Rainy Night and Day

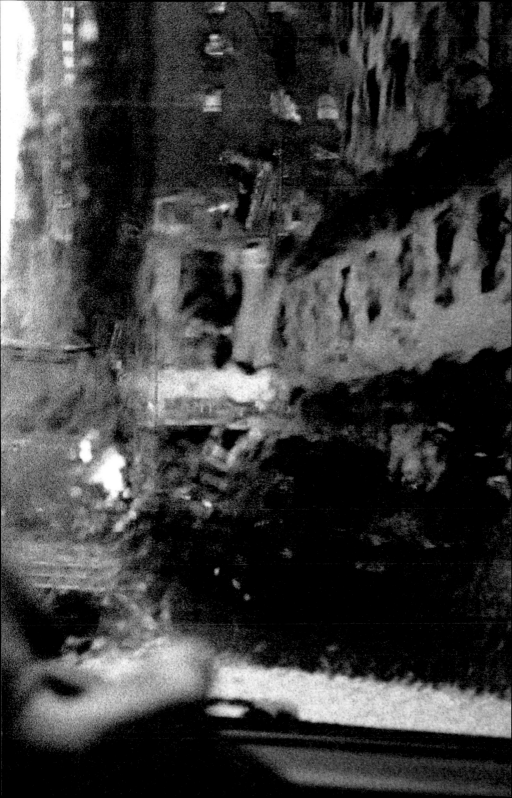

Home Through the Heart of the World
With David Bradford to the End of a Day's Work

The dollar bills rustle. The dollar bills always rustle when he sticks them in his shirt pocket. One fare, one rustle. And again now, as he sets down the well-dressed gentleman at Grand Central on the corner of 26th Street and Park Avenue South. Five dollars something.

The man says, "Otherwise I've only got large bills. If it had cost more, I would have had to give you quarters." Rather not, although David replies, "As long as it's American currency, no problem."

The man goes to work. David Bradford thinks about his break. It's nearly time. He's been out and about for five hours. It's nine o'clock in the morning. The sun rose almost two-and-a-half hours ago. David's taxi came along 57th Street, towards the East River. The sky was grayish-blue, streaked with the pale morning light. It was an experience. Sunrise in New York is often an experience.

Today he's already been driving to and fro between downtown and Upper West Side for hours, looking for a fare. Tried out all the night clubs, then hoped for the first businesspeople whom he might have caught on the way to the airport. Then from 7 a.m. past Grand Central as always, where the commuters drift in. Business was bad, and at such times, David often has no eye for the fascination of New York. "If you have a fare," he says, "everything's fine. Otherwise your eye roves restlessly across the streets." And then he has no time for photography.

From 26th Street across to Madison Avenue. A woman gets in. David sets the meter going. Two dollars basic for the first fifth of a mile, thirty cents for each additional fifth of a mile. A drive across twenty-five blocks in a north-south direction costs about six dollars fifty. Night supplement: fifty cents. Each time he sets the meter, there's this stupid taped announcement to fasten your seat belt. It can be heard in every New York taxi, spoken by a series of celebrities from Placido Domingo to the coach of the New York Yankees. In David's cab it's the well-known sexologist Dr. Ruth Westheimer. "Buckle up," growls the old lady. David says, "This announcement drives me crazy. If you hear that all day long, you go meshuga."

"How's business?" asks the lady who's just got in. "Okay," says David. "Where d'you want to go?" The woman wants to go somewhere in midtown. And David asks, "Where do you work?"

The woman works for a food company which tries out products for the Latin American market in its test kitchen. Hamburgers, tacos, hot dogs. They carry on talking. The woman once cooked for the French ambassador. She says, "I chat away to everyone, I have to get everything off my chest." And then she explains that her family has been in New York for 208 years, but that she has never been to Staten Island, that every Russian immigrant over 60 is a pickpocket, and that her husband works in the perfume trade. "He's got what they call a nose. To make up for it, he doesn't talk so much. We're a perfect couple."

Back to Grand Central. Men in trenchcoats and carrying briefcases hurry along the sidewalks. A white stretch limousine is parked by the side of the road. Two men get in. Dark glasses. "They look like Mafia," says David in jest. Two black women jump out on to the street from between two vans. They wave, David stops. Another fare. They want to go uptown. Not bad, that'll bring in a few dollars at least. David switches the radio on. FM 88.3. They're playing a piece by jazz trumpeter Chet Baker. David says, "I would've preferred to play the trumpet. The trumpet is an instrument for people with solo talent. But then I was forced to take up the trombone after all."

What's left is a solo on the steering wheel. Just him and the taxi, eleven hours a day in the concrete labyrinth, sometimes twelve. Without his daily break, David wouldn't manage. About ten, he drives home. Chelsea. He parks his taxi and goes to his apartment. It looks a bit like a photographer's studio with hundreds of contact prints hanging on the walls. He makes himself a cocktail of vegetables. Beetroot, celery and parsley. Relaxes a little, maybe half an hour, forty-five minutes. Then it's back on the road.

11:30 a.m. The next customer gets in on Broadway by 85th Street. He's wearing a gray camel coat, and he's in a hurry. "Did you take these pictures," he asks. David says yes, passes back his portfolio. "They're very good," says the man, adding, "Funny. Taxi drivers are a special kind. Do you know the book by Nik Cohn, *The Heart of the World*? That's about a New York taxi driver, too."

In *The Heart of the World* Nik Cohn tells of a walk along Broadway. The book is based on a true story. Actually Cohn, a successful scriptwriter who made his name with *Saturday Night Fever*, had wanted to travel round the world. But a friend persuaded him to explore Broadway from the Battery up to the Bronx. Broadway still follows the route the Algonquin Indians used to get across Manhattan. The Indians called it the "Great White Way". Cohn's friend said it was a world in itself.

The taxi makes its way with difficulty through a jam at Columbus Circle, with Central Park to the left, through a canyon of buildings with illuminated facades. Blinking, radiant with light, flooded with pedestrians and vehicles, Times Square appears. The man in back says, "Isn't this square always fascinating?" And to David, "You can reckon you're lucky to experience this a dozen times a day – morning, noon and night." David says, "I love Broadway. Here I would even have liked to take some color photos."

The man says, "No good." David says, "Maybe you're right. Everything would look like candy." The man says, "New York is only colorful on the surface. In reality the city is black-and-white. One single contrast." 12:45. Still almost two hours to go. The great hero in *The Heart of the World* is not the narrator, but a taxi-driver called Sasha Zim. Zim is one of those crazy types who do nothing all day but drive, drive, drive. And at night he sleeps in a tenement next to his drums. Sometimes he sleeps in the taxi, because the drumset, thinks Zim, needs its peace and quiet. Somewhere in the book, Zim writes, *"...Is Broadway and who would not know what that means? ...each intersection with another avenue ... sparks different interaction. Each of sparks generates own brilliance, which may flare briefly or lengthily, may fade or may burn once again. Broadway, in all euphoria, is Yellow Brick Road, one that seductively promises, but doesn't guarantee, Emerald City at road's end."*

A young woman gets in. David drives down Broadway. Past Herald Square, 34th Street. The neighborhood is known as Little Korea. Behind it is the demolition area in front of Union Square. It belongs to what is still called the Garment District, where cloth used to be produced and clothing sewn. Through SoHo, which has grown chic in the past twenty years, and is now crowded round the clock with people on shopping or drinking sprees. Past Little Italy across Canal Street. Sidewalk traders everywhere, selling imitation Prada handbags, sweatshirts and fake Rolex watches. Round the corner is Chinatown.

The young woman says, "You can put me down up there on the right." And, "Have you seen the paper yet? In my apartment house, someone jumped out the window yesterday." David says, "Interesting. Do they know why he jumped?" The young woman says, "No idea. Too many crazy people in this city."

It's now 2 p.m. David leaves Broadway, heads for the World Trade Center. In a narrow alley, a fat girl gets in. David tries to strike up a conversation with her. She doesn't want to talk. When he's set her down, David says, "There are people who seal themselves off from the surrounding world like a tank."

He's had enough, wants to get back to the garage. But on the corner ahead a man is waving. Beside him there's a pile of cartons. David helps him load. The man gets in and says, "What have I done to deserve this? I stop the only taxi driver in New York who speaks English." David grins. He produces his set piece. "There's a surcharge for that, you know." The man says, "I'll pay it gladly." Another pleasant drive before the day's work comes to an end.

The man pays. Rustling in the shirt pocket. David doesn't yet know how much he's earned. He never counts his money while he's driving. He thinks it could be 200 dollars, probably less. That would be about 80 dollars net for 12 hours work. David helps the man unload. Helps him carry the cartons into a backyard. The man says, "For me, taxi drivers are the unsung heroes of this city. Without them, nothing here would work. I just don't know why they're hated by everyone."

David drives back to the garage. It's 2:37 p.m. At the office he hands in the form where he's noted the details of every journey: time, distance and fare. He exchanges a few words with the dispatcher, who reserves for him the Medallion with the number 6K23 for the next day. Of course. David is one of the garage's regulars. His partner will turn up in a few minutes. They'll maybe chat a bit between the Coke machine and the parked cars. Suddenly David Bradford says, "I simply can't imagine ever not being a New York taxi driver."

Durchs Herz der Welt nach Hause
Mit David Bradford bis ans Ende einer Dienstfahrt

Die Dollarnoten rascheln. Immer rascheln die Dollarnoten, wenn er sie sich in die Hemdtasche steckt. Jede Fuhre einmal Rascheln. Jetzt wieder, als er den gut gekleideten Herrn absetzt, Grand Central bis Ecke 26th Street und Park Avenue South. Fünf Dollar irgendwas.

Der Mann sagt: „Ich habe sonst nur noch große Scheine. Wenn es mehr gekostet hätte, hätte ich Ihnen Quarter geben müssen." Besser nicht, obwohl David antwortet: „Solange es amerikanische Währung ist, kein Problem."

Der Mann geht zur Arbeit, David Bradford denkt an seine Pause. Langsam wird es Zeit. Er ist seit über fünf Stunden unterwegs. Es ist neun Uhr morgens. Vor knapp zweieinhalb Stunden ist die Sonne aufgegangen. Davids Taxi kam die 57th Street entlang, fuhr Richtung East River. Graublau war der Himmel, durchzogen von fahlem Morgenlicht. Es war ein Erlebnis. Sonnenaufgang in New York ist oft ein Erlebnis.

Heute ist er bereits stundenlang auf der Suche nach Passagieren zwischen Downtown und Upper West Side hin- und hergegondelt. Er hat alle Nachtclubs abgeklappert, dann auf die ersten Geschäftsleute gehofft, die er auf dem Weg zum Flughafen hätte abfangen können, ab sieben Uhr morgens immer wieder vorbei am Grand Central, wo die Pendler eintrudeln. Das Geschäft lief nicht gut, und dann hat David für die Faszination

New Yorks oft kein Auge. „Wenn man eine Fuhre hat", sagt er, „ist alles in Ordnung, ansonsten kreuzt der Blick rastlos durch die Straßen." Dann hat er auch keine Muße zu fotografieren.

Von der 26th rüber zur Madison Avenue. Eine Frau steigt zu. David stellt den Zähler an. 2 Dollar Grundgebühr für die erste Fünftelmeile, für jede weitere 30 Cent. Eine Fahrt über 25 Blocks in Nord-Süd-Richtung kostet etwa 6 Dollar 50. Nachtaufschlag: 50 Cent. Jedesmal, wenn er den Zähler anstellt, läuft diese doofe Ansage vom Band, daß man sich anschnallen soll. Die läuft in jedem New Yorker Taxi, gesprochen von einer Reihe von Prominenten, von Placido Domingo bis zum Baseballtrainer der New York Yankees. In Davids Wagen ist es die berühmte Sexualforscherin Dr. Ruth Westheimer. „Buckle up", schnarrt die alte Dame. David sagt: „Diese Ansage macht mich noch wahnsinnig. Wenn man das den ganzen Tag hört, wird man meschugge."

„Wie läuft das Geschäft?" will die gerade zugestiegene Frau wissen. „Okay", sagt David, „wo wollen Sie hin?" Die Frau will irgendwo nach Midtown, und David fragt: „Wo arbeiten Sie?"

Die Frau arbeitet für einen Lebensmittelkonzern, der in seinen Versuchsküchen Produkte für den lateinamerikanischen Markt testet. Hamburger, Tacos, Hot Dogs. Man unterhält sich. Die Frau hat mal für den französischen Botschafter gekocht. Sie sagt: „Ich quatsche immer mit jedem, muß immer alles loswerden." Und dann erzählt sie noch, daß ihre Familie seit 208 Jahren in New York ansässig ist, sie aber noch nie auf Staten Island war, daß jeder russische Immigrant über 60 ein Taschendieb sei und ihr Mann im 'Parfümbusiness' arbeite. „Er hat das, was man eine Nase nennt. Dafür redet er nicht so viel. Wir sind ein perfektes Paar."

Zurück zum Grand Central. Männer in Trenchcoats und mit Aktentaschen hetzen über die Gehsteige. Am Straßenrand parkt eine weiße Stretchlimousine. Zwei Männer steigen ein, Sonnenbrillen. „Die sehen aus wie von der Mafia", scherzt David. Zwischen zwei Kleintransportern springen zwei schwarze Frauen auf die Straße, winken. David hält an. Wieder eine Fuhre. Es geht Richtung Uptown. Nicht schlecht, da kommen wenigstens ein paar Dollar zusammen. David schaltet das Radio an. FM 88.3. Sie spielen ein Lied des Jazztrompeters Chet Baker. David sagt: „Ich hätte eigentlich auch lieber Trompete gespielt, Trompete ist ein Instrument für Leute mit solistischem Talent. Aber dann wurde ich doch zur Posaune gezwungen."

Geblieben ist ein Solo am Lenkrad. Nur er und das Taxi. Elf Stunden täglich im Betonlabyrinth, manchmal zwölf. Ohne seine tägliche Pause würde David es nicht schaffen. Gegen zehn fährt er nach Hause, Stadtteil Chelsea, stellt sein Taxi ab und geht in seine Wohnung, die ein bißchen aussieht wie ein Fotostudio mit hunderten von

Kontaktbögen, die an den Wänden hängen. Er macht sich einen Gemüsecocktail aus Rote Beete, Sellerie und Petersilie, entspannt sich ein bißchen, vielleicht eine halbe Stunde, 45 Minuten, dann wieder zurück auf die Straße.

11.30 Uhr. Der nächste Kunde steigt am Broadway ein, Höhe 85th Street. Er trägt einen Kamelhaarmantel und hat es eilig. „Haben Sie diese Bilder gemacht?" fragt er. David bejaht, reicht sein Portfolio nach hinten. „Die sind sehr gut", sagt der Mann und ergänzt: „Komisch, Taxifahrer sind eine besondere Spezies. Kennen Sie das Buch von Nik Cohn? Das Herz der Welt. Da geht es auch um einen Taxifahrer in New York."

In *Das Herz der Welt* erzählt Nik Cohn von einem Spaziergang über den Broadway. Das Buch basiert auf einer wahren Begebenheit. Eigentlich hatte Cohn, ein erfolgreicher Dreh-buchautor und bekannt geworden mit dem Script zu *Saturday Night Fever*, eine Weltreise machen wollen, doch ein Freund überredete ihn dazu, den Broadway von der Battery bis hinauf in Richtung Bronx zu erkunden. Der Broadway verläuft immer noch auf der Route, auf der die Algonquin-Indianer Manhattan durchwandert haben. Die Indianer nannten ihn „Großer Weißer Weg". Cohns Freund meinte: „Das ist eine Welt für sich."

Das Taxi quält sich durch den Stau am Columbus Circle, links der Central Park, in Fahrtrichtung davor ein Canyon von Gebäuden mit illuminierten Fassaden. Blinkend, leuchtend, von Verkehr und Passanten überflutet, taucht der Times Square auf. Der Mann im Fond sagt: „Ist dieser Platz nicht immer wieder faszinierend?" Und zu David: „Sie können sich glücklich schätzen, das jeden Tag dutzende Male erleben zu können – morgens, mittags, abends, nachts." David sagt: „Ich liebe den Broadway. Hier hätte ich manchmal meine Bilder gerne in Farbe geschossen."

Der Mann sagt: „Keine gute Idee." David sagt: „Vielleicht haben Sie recht, dann würde alles aussehen wie ein Bonbon." Der Mann sagt: „New York ist nur an der Oberfläche bunt, in Wirklichkeit ist die Stadt schwarz-weiß, ein einziger Kontrast." 12.45 Uhr. Noch knapp zwei Stunden bis Feierabend.

Der große Held in *Das Herz der Welt* ist nicht der Erzähler, sondern ein Taxifahrer namens Sasha Zim. Zim ist einer dieser Irren, die den ganzen Tag nichts anderes tun als fahren, fahren, fahren, und nachts schläft er in einer Baracke neben einem Schlagzeug. Manchmal schläft er auch im Taxi, weil das Schlagzeug, wie Zim meint, Ruhe brauche. Zim sagt in dem Buch einmal: „...Ist der Broadway, und wer weiß nicht, was das bedeutet? An jeder Kreuzung mit anderer Straße schlagen neue Funken. Jeder Funke leuchtet anders, leuchtet kurz oder lang, verlöscht oder flammt wieder auf. Für alle, die hoffen, ist der Broadway die Straße der Verheißung, wo am Ende das Eldorado lockt, was es vielleicht nicht gibt." Eine junge Frau steigt ein. David fährt den Broadway hin-unter. Vorbei am Herald Square, 34th Street. Man nennt das Viertel Little Korea.

Dahinter kommt die abgerissene Gegend vor dem Union Square. Sie gehört noch zum sogenannten Garment District, wo früher in Fabriken Stoffe produziert und Kleider genäht wurden. Durch SoHo, das chic geworden ist in den letzten zwanzig Jahren und inzwischen rund um die Uhr überlaufen von Menschen auf Einkaufs- oder Kneipentour. Vorbei an Little Italy über die Canal Street. Überall fliegende Händler, die Imitate von Prada-Handtaschen, Sweatshirts und gefälschte Rolexuhren feilbieten. Um die Ecke liegt Chinatown.

Die junge Frau sagt: „Da vorne rechts können Sie mich rauslassen." Und: „Haben Sie schon die Zeitung gelesen? In meinem Haus ist nämlich gestern Nacht jemand aus dem Fenster gesprungen." David sagt: „Interessant. Weiß man, warum er gesprungen ist?" Die junge Frau sagt: „Keine Ahnung. Zu viele Verrückte in dieser Stadt."

Inzwischen ist es 14 Uhr. David verläßt den Broadway, steuert Richtung World Trade Center. In einer kleinen Gasse steigt ein dickes Mädchen zu. David versucht mit ihr ins Gespräch zu kommen. Sie will sich nicht unterhalten. Als er sie abgesetzt hat, sagt David: „Es gibt Menschen, die schotten sich von ihrer Umwelt ab wie ein Panzer."

Er hat genug, will zurück in die Garage. Doch vorne an der Ecke winkt ein Mann. Neben ihm Stapel von Kartons. David hilft ihm beim Einladen. Der Mann steigt ein, sagt: „Womit habe ich dieses Glück verdient? Erwische ich doch glatt den einzigen Taxifahrer New Yorks, der Englisch spricht." David schmunzelt. Jetzt kommt sein Standardspruch. „Sie wissen, dafür müssen Sie Zuschlag bezahlen." Der Mann sagt: „Mache ich doch gerne." Nochmal eine angenehme Tour, bevor eine weitere Dienstfahrt zu Ende geht.

Der Mann bezahlt. Rascheln in der Hemdtasche. David weiß noch nicht, wieviel er verdient hat. Er zählt nie sein Geld, während er fährt. Er meint, es könnten vielleicht 200 Dollar sein, wahrscheinlich weniger. Das wäre ein Nettoverdienst von etwa 80 Dollar für zwölf Stunden. David hilft dem Mann beim Ausladen, hilft ihm, die Kartons in einen Hinterhof zu schleppen. Der Mann sagt: „Taxifahrer sind für mich die unbesungenen Helden dieser Stadt. Ohne sie würde hier gar nichts funktionieren. Ich weiß überhaupt nicht, warum sie von allen gehaßt werden."

David fährt zurück zur Garage. Es ist 14.37 Uhr. Er gibt im Büro das Formular ab, auf dem er jede Fahrt samt Uhrzeit, Wegstrecke und Fahrpreis notiert hat. Wechselt ein paar Worte mit dem Dispatcher, der ihm für den nächsten Tag wieder das Medallion mit der Nummer 6K23 reserviert. Logisch, David gehört zur festen Belegschaft des Ladens. Sein Partner wird in ein paar Minuten auftauchen, sie werden vielleicht zwischen Cola-Automat und geparkten Wagen ein wenig plaudern. Plötzlich sagt David Bradford: „Ich kann mir gar nicht vorstellen, irgendwann einmal kein New Yorker Taxifahrer mehr zu sein."

Rentrer chez soi en traversant le cœur du monde
Avec David Bradford jusqu'à la fin de son service

Les dollars bruissent. Les dollars bruissent toujours quand il les glisse dans la pochette de sa chemise. Pour chaque course, un bruissement. Ainsi qu'au moment où il dépose l'homme bien habillé qu'il a conduit de Grand Central jusqu'à l'angle de 26ᵉ Rue et de Park Avenue Sud. Environ 5 dollars. L'homme dit : « A part cela, je n'ai plus que des gros billets. Si la course avait coûté plus cher, j'aurais dû vous donner des quarters. » Vaut mieux pas, pense David, mais il répond : « Tant que c'est de l'argent américain, pas de problème. »

L'homme se rend à son travail, David Bradford pense à sa pause. Ça commence à lui sembler long. Il est en route depuis plus de cinq heures. Il est neuf heures du matin. Il y a à peine deux heures et demie que le soleil s'est levé. Le taxi de David descendait la 57ᵉ Rue, roulant en direction de l'East River. Le ciel était gris bleu, teinté de la lueur blafarde de l'aurore. Une sensation unique. Le lever du soleil sur New York a souvent un caractère exceptionnel.

Aujourd'hui, il a déjà fait la navette pendant des heures entre Downtown et Upper West Side en quête de passagers. Après avoir fait toutes les sorties de bars et boîtes de nuits, puis espéré croiser les premiers hommes d'affaires qu'il aurait pu intercepter en route vers l'aéroport, il n'a cessé de repasser devant Grand Central où, à partir de sept heures du matin, les banlieusards arrivent en masse. Les affaires ne marchent pas fort, et, dans ces moments-là, David devient indifférent à la fascination de New York. « Quand on a une course, dit-il, tout va bien. Sinon, les yeux sondent frénétiquement les rues. » Et alors, bien sûr, il n'a même pas le temps de prendre de photos.

De la 26ᵉ en direction de Madison Avenue. Une femme monte dans le taxi. David met le compteur à zéro. 2 dollars de taxe de base pour le premier cinquième de mile, puis 30 cents pour chaque cinquième suivant. Un trajet de 25 pâtés de maisons dans le sens nord-sud coûte environ 6,50 dollars. Supplément de nuit : 50 cents. Chaque fois qu'il remet son compteur à zéro, il entend inlassablement ce message stupide sur cassette, qui vous intime d'attacher votre ceinture. Il est diffusé dans chaque taxi new-yorkais, prononcé par toute une série de célébrités allant de Placido Domingo à l'entraîneur de base-ball des New York Yankees. Dans la voiture de David, on peut entendre la célèbre sexologue Ruth Westheimer. « Buckle up », déclare la vieille dame d'une voix de crécelle. David déclare : « Ce message va me rendre complètement fou. Quand on entend ça toute la journée, on en a vraiment ras le bol. »

« Comment vont les affaires ? », veut savoir la femme qui vient de monter. « Comme ci, comme ça, dit David. Vous allez où ? » La femme veut se rendre quelque part à Midtown, et David lui demande : « Et où travaillez-vous ? » La femme travaille pour un groupe alimentaire qui teste dans ses cuisines-laboratoires des produits destinés au marché latino-américain : hamburgers, tacos, hot dogs. On parle de choses et d'autres. La femme a jadis travaillé comme cuisinière chez l'ambassadeur de France. Elle déclare : « Je bavarde toujours avec tout le monde, j'ai toujours un tas de choses à dire. » Et, alors, elle raconte que sa famille est établie à New York depuis 208 ans, mais qu'elle ne s'est encore jamais rendue à Staten Island, que chaque immigrant russe âgé de plus de 60 ans est un pickpocket et que son mari travaille « dans le business de la parfumerie ». « Il a ce qu'il est convenu d'appeler un nez. En revanche, il n'est pas très bavard. Nous sommes un couple parfait. »

De retour à Grand Central. Des hommes en trench-coat portant un attaché-case sprintent sur les trottoirs. Une limousine blanche d'une longueur inouïe est garée au bord de la rue. Deux hommes montent à bord, lunettes de soleil. « Ils ressemblent à des mafiosi », dit David en blaguant. Entre deux petites camionnettes, deux types surgissent soudain dans la rue, le hèlent. David s'arrête. Encore une course. Cap sur Uptown. Pas mal, cela va au moins lui rapporter quelques dollars. David allume la radio. FM 88.3. On entend un morceau du trompettiste de jazz Chet Baker. David déclare : « En fait, j'aurais moi aussi préféré jouer de la trompette. La trompette est un instrument pour les gens qui ont un talent de soliste. Mais j'ai été contraint de jouer du trombone. » Ce qui lui est resté, c'est le solo au volant. Juste lui et le taxi. Onze heures par jour dans un labyrinthe en béton, parfois 12 heures. Sans sa pause quotidienne, David n'y arriverait pas. Vers dix heures, il rentre chez lui, dans le quartier de Chelsea, gare son taxi et rentre dans son appartement qui ressemble un peu à un studio de photo avec des centaines de contacts accrochés aux murs. Il se fait un cocktail de légumes à base de betteraves rouges, céleri et persil, se détend un peu, une demi-heure, peut-être trois quarts d'heure, puis redescend dans la rue.

11 heures 30. Le prochain client monte à Broadway, à la hauteur de la 85e Rue. Il porte un manteau en poils de chameau et il est très pressé. « C'est vous qui avez fait ces photos ? » demande-t-il. David acquiesce, lui passe son press-book. « Elles sont très bonnes », dit l'homme avant d'ajouter : « C'est bizarre, les chauffeurs de taxi sont une espèce particulière. Vous connaissez le livre de Nik Cohn *Le cœur du monde* ? Il y est aussi question d'un chauffeur de taxi new- yorkais. »Dans *Le Cœur du monde*, Nik Cohn raconte une promenade le long de Broadway. Le livre est inspiré d'un fait réel. A l'origine, Cohn, un scénariste à succès qui est aussi devenu célèbre avec le script de *Saturday Night Fever*, avait voulu faire un voyage autour du monde, mais l'un de ses amis l'a convaincu de partir explorer Broadway, de Battery en remontant en direction du Bronx. Broadway suit aujourd'hui encore la route qu'empruntaient les Indiens Algonquin quand ils traversaient Manhattan à pied. Les Indiens l'appelaient le « Grand Sentier blanc ». L'ami de Cohn s'exprime en ces mots : « C'est un monde en soi ».

Le taxi progresse à une lenteur désespérante dans les embouteillages de Columbus Circle, à gauche, Central Park, avec, avant, dans le sens de la marche, un canyon de gratte-ciel aux façades illuminées. Clignotant, scintillant, envahi par le flot de la circulation et des passants, Times Square apparaît enfin. L'homme assis sur la banquette arrière s'exclame : « Cette place n'est-elle pas à chaque fois fascinante ? » Et, s'adressant à David : « Vous pouvez vous estimer heureux d'assister à ce spectacle des douzaines de fois par jour – le matin, le midi, le soir, la nuit. » David acquiesce : « J'adore Broadway. Ici, j'aurais parfois bien aimé faire des photos en couleur. »L'homme dit : « Ce serait pas génial. » David rétorque : « Peut-être avez-vous raison, tout ressemblerait alors à un bon-bon. » L'homme ajoute : « La ville de New York n'est colorée qu'en surface, en réalité, la ville est en noir et blanc, un seul et unique contraste. » 12 heures 45. Dans moins de deux heures, David aura fini sa journée.

Le véritable héros dans *Le Cœur du monde* n'est pas le narrateur, mais un chauffeur de taxi du nom de Sasha Zim. Zim est l'un de ces fous qui ne font rien d'autre de toute la journée que de rouler, rouler, rouler et, la nuit, il dort dans une baraque à côté de sa bat-terie. Il lui arrive aussi de dormir dans son taxi, parce que la batterie, comme le prétend Zim, a besoin de calme. Dans le livre, Zim déclare un jour : « Ça s'appelle Broadway, et qui ne saurait pas ce que ça veut dire. À chaque carrefour, une autre rue, une nouvelle luminosité d'une intensité différente, une luminosité qui faiblit ou se ravive. Pour tous ceux qui espèrent en quelque chose, Broadway est la rue synonyme de promesse, celle qui conduit à un eldorado qui peut-être n'existe pas. »

Une jeune femme monte dans le taxi. David descend Broadway. Longeant Herald Square, 34ᵉ Rue. On appelle ce quartier la Little Corea. Derrière lui se trouve le quartier en démolition d'Union Square. Il fait partie de ce que l'on appelle Garment District où, jadis, on fabriquait des tissus dans des usines et cousait des vêtements. À travers SoHo, qui est devenu à la mode ces 20 dernières années et est, entre-temps, envahi 24 heures sur 24 par des gens qui font du shopping ou la tournée des grands ducs. Longe Little Italy de l'autre côté de Canal Street. Partout, des commerçants à la sauvette qui cherchent à vous refiler des contrefaçons de sacs à main Prada, des sweat-shirts et de fausses montres Rolex. Juste à l'angle se trouve Chinatown.

La jeune femme dit : « Vous pouvez me déposer au coin là-bas à droite ». Et ajoute : « Vous avez déjà lu le journal ? Figurez-vous que, dans mon immeuble, la nuit dernière, quelqu'un a sauté par la fenêtre. » David dit : « Intéressant. On sait pourquoi la personne a sauté ? » La jeune femme dit : « Aucune idée. Il y a trop de fous dans cette ville. » Il est déjà 14 heures. David quitte Broadway, prend la direction du World Trade Center. Dans une petite allée, une grosse fille monte dans son taxi. David essaie d'engager la conversation. Mais la fille reste taciturne. Après l'avoir déposée, David dit : « Il y a des gens comme ça qui se coupent du monde, comme s'ils vivaient dans une coquille. »

Il en a assez, veut rentrer au garage. Mais, là-bas, au coin, un homme lui fait signe. À côté de lui s'entassent des cartons. David l'aide à les charger. L'homme monte et lui dit : « Qu'est-ce qui m'a valu cette chance ? Et je tombe même sur le seul chauffeur de taxi new-yorkais qui parle anglais. » David sourit d'aise. Il peut de nouveau jouer de sa réplique standard. « Vous savez, il va vous falloir payer un supplément pour ça. » L'homme lui dit : « Mais volontiers. » Encore une course agréable avant de finir la journée.

L'homme paie. Bruissement dans la poche de sa chemise. David ne sait pas encore combien il a gagné. Il ne compte jamais son argent pendant qu'il travaille. Il pense qu'il a peut-être 200 dollars, probablement moins. Ce serait un gain net de 80 dollars pour 12 heures. David aide l'homme à décharger, l'aide à transporter les cartons dans une arrière-cour. L'homme lui dit : « Pour moi, les chauffeurs de taxi sont les héros anonymes de cette ville. Sans eux, absolument rien ne fonctionnerait ici. Je ne sais vraiment pas pourquoi tout le monde les hait. » David rentre au garage. Il est 14 heures 37. Au bureau, il remet le formulaire sur lequel il a noté chaque course avec l'heure, le trajet et le prix. Il échange quelques mots avec le dispatcher qui lui a de nouveau réservé pour le lendemain la Medallion avec le numéro 6 K 23. C'est logique, David fait partie des meubles dans cette entreprise. Son partenaire va faire son apparition dans quelques minutes, ils vont peut-être échanger quelques mots entre le distributeur de cocas et les voitures garées. Soudain, David Bradford déclare : « Je ne peux absolument pas m'imaginer ne plus être un jour chauffeur de taxi new-yorkais. »

Snow, Day and Night